ISBN: 978-1-312-78842-8

D1810676

The Depth of the Drop:

Zen Rap on the Shobogenzo

Volume 2:

The rat is time, the tiger is time

"The depth of the drop is the height of the moon.
As for the duration of the reflection, you must examine
The water's vastness or smallness,
And you must discern the brightness or dimness
Of the heavenly moon."

Eihei Dogen

This second volume is also dedicated to:

Robert Aitken Roshi, my Zen Teacher, Friend and Companion

Maezumi Roshi, in the memories of the beautiful and creative moments shared in the Dokusan Room as well as in the Genjo Koan of everyday life situations.

Truly it is also dedicated to my first teacher, the Monk Yuan Chueh.

And to the teacher Fernando Annetta, for the initial kick start.

To the sistahs and bruddahs of Hawaii Aina,
To Dougo, for the long time deep friendship and inspiration, the shared cigars and muzik, the Lanai talk story, and the ocean sitting times…
To Paulo, heart friend who visited Latino Aina, for his brotherhood and inspiration…
To Red Flea, for the friendship, hug and presence, and the shared muzik and poetry…
To Vince the Algarrobo Man who wandered around Latino Aina and La Quebrada…

And to Mark, Caroline all-ways an inspiration in the Dharma DanceStruggle), Laulani (For the seed of Aloha Revolution), Maleko a true "Lost & found" brother), the waves, tides, clouds, mountains, rains, Brother Gecko Aumakua and the horizon.

To the "Zen Gang", the latencies I trust as I deeply trust the seeds and spores: Claire, Daniel, Dario…. Tash and Jill…

And to my love and life companion, Janet

My stepson Emiliano, whose wonderful love of life made him a survivor of two lungs transplant, and a constant inspiration (no pun intended…)

To my daughters Elina and Aruna, the wings and arrows of life flying forth…
And my grandson Etienne who is walking this Mother Earth fresh…

To my Zapatista friend, brother and inspiration Guillermo Michel Sinner, who no longer walks on this wounded earth…

To all the Originary Peoples of the earth, deep thanks from the heart for keeping the Memory and Wisdom of Mother Earth, the womb and cradle of true Zen understanding, expression and walking.

4

To the brothers and sisters of the Zapatista movement, for building the New World step by step with poetry, laughter and strength, and keeping the sparks of Digniry and Original Heart alive and shining against the deadly works of ignorance, hate and greed.

At last but not at least, I share this book and words as an invitation to dance against the hegemony of sadness of the imperial powers of ignorance and greed....

Cheers!!! Salud!!!

About the Rapper:

The Augusto Alcalde I know has many manifestations.
Martial Arts master and motorcyclist, Chinese medicine practitioner and indigenous peoples' activist, Zen roshi and jester, musician and writer.
When I think of the many forms he takes on the singular path he walks, I think of a story told about the Buddha.

One day, Buddha and his disciple Ananda were walking with their begging bowls. Buddha asked Ananda, "Ananda, do you know the essence of my teaching?"
Ananda, who had followed the Buddha for most of his life, and whose memory was faultless, said, "Yes, Most Honored One. The essence of your teaching is the Eightfold Path."
"No, it is not," Buddha said.
Surprised, Ananda tried again. And again and again and again.
Yet to every answer he gave out of his perfect memory of Enlightened One's teachings, Buddha said, "No, it is not."
Finally, Ananda could think of nothing else.
"Please reveal the ultimate truth to me, Most Honored One. I will remember and pass it on to everyone who will listen."
"Very good, Ananda.
I hereby trust the ultimate truth of my teaching to you. It is this: Be a friend.
There is no greater attainment in this life or lives to come than to be a friend."

During the twenty years I have known Augusto, through good times and bad, he has always been my friend.
In this book of translations and commentaries, you will find he is your friend, too.

Takashi Matsuoka

Writer, Zen and Martial Arts practitioner
Author of "Cloud of Sparrows" and "Autumn Bridge"

Oahu-Hawaii- Niu Valley

What from an Old Buddha dies, is not the Old Buddha...
(In the memory and presence of Robert Aitken)

Heard Roshi died, and i send a heartfelt Hug and gassho to the friends.
And i write to him from my heart full of gratitude

Dear Roshi:

I remember the 40th anniversary of the Diamond Sangha, when i was there.
I remember it with good and deep memories of the place, the group, the Aina
and your presence and teaching and interaction
in the Dokusan room for so many years.

And i want to express my gratitude to you for that and your help in so many ways
during those years that i appreciate and cherish so much, and have left so many
teachings and memories in my heart and my walking. Deep thanks.
No doubt what you started as the Diamond Sangha will echo in time forever, and
i hope will be a good seed for the new horizon that is
so badly needed these days in this wounded earth.

I remember Koko An and Manoa Valley, as well as Palolo and the times we
shared together. I remember, and feel grateful to life for them.

And i remember you quoting:
"A monk asked Ta-lung, "What is the 'minutely subtle?'"
Ta-lung said, "The breeze brings the voice of the water close to my pillow;
the moon carries the shadow of the mountain near to my couch."

And indeed this breeze here in distant Cordoba City brings the voice of the
gecko, of the bells, and the smell of the Dojo so close that
seems the ocean is right here in the backyard.

I also remember you saying:
Ta-lung said, "The mountain flowers bloom like brocade;
/ the river between the hills is blue as indigo."

I do not know about the mountain flowers blooming, neither i do about the river between the hills, i have so much to walk and lean that maybe for the 100th anniversary i will be able to say i know something.

But i do know in my heart the meaning and importance in my life and walking of your presence and the Diamond Sangha
in those days we walked together the Dharma Aina.

I offer heartfelt and deep mahalo nui loa, respect,
gratitude and love to you for all this.

Aloha O'e
A hui hou kakou
Nine bows.

Augusto Alcalde

 *Zen is to walk the Dream*

Post-liminar words…

"I see words beyond any acceptable meaning, this is how i express my dreaming." says the Aboriginal Poet of the Land or the Rainbow Snake (Australia) Lionel Fogarty.

The words you are about to walk here are not written in English.
Neither are they written in Spanish.
Neither are they translated from one language to another.

Zen is to walk the Dream, to walk and express the new horizon and heart so badly needed in our Land, this wounded Mother Earth.

And this dreaming asks, requires, and needs something, in the expression of the writing, in the expression of the reading, in the expression of the true walking; she needs that *"seeing beyond any acceptable meaning"*.
This is what I want to touch and share here, as you, we, walk through the words.

To call this seeing in some or any way, is to lose the dreaming that creates the poetic act that heals and revolutionize the heart and the world.

I ask then humbly to walk in this Wind and this Seed with no concepts like the ones of wisdom or ignorance, good or bad, Zen or non Zen… of English or Spanish, or even of poetry, less even the ideas of grammar and spelling.

Even less the ones about "acceptable meaning…"

It is here and offering, an intent of rhythm, an intent of chord, an intent of dream, in hope of an echo.

This one that writes does not write more than the one that reads.
"The word is half of the one who says it, and half of the one that hears it", do say the Zapatista brothers and sisters…

The History writes, the Burning Memory writes, writes the ordinary of the road, the loss, the love, the elusive and unpredictable revolution that happens moment to moment.
And without them, I believe deep in my heart and walking, there is no Zen.

Writes the Certainty, the Hope writes, the morrow writes.
And it is a walking, where *"asking questions we walk"*.

There is no order among this texts, neither date nor place (in general…), yes there is blood, there are tears, there is dance and there is happiness and joy. There is Love.

As the disposition and the act of seeing and walking beyond acceptable meanings, the Wind in the Seed, the heart and heartbeat, heartwalk of Zen.

Wind and Seed that awakens the Heart of everyday reality; the need of a renovation of the word.
And the intimate connection with the Land and the Culture.

Poetry and rhythm and Zen become then Heart to Heart Oral Tradition, and there is no poet or "zennist", only that mistery (like "mist") that dreams in the one that writes and in the one that reads.

I employ thus the Spanish against the Spanish, the English against the English. The Land and the Culture do not respond to grammatical laws, her word responds much more to Primal Rhythms, the ones of the Original Peoples, of the stones, mountains, rivers, animals and plants.

Culture that is Identity and enbrothering step.

Writin' walkin' poetry, words and Zen for the Horizon.
For freedom from the cultural colonialism of the word and the symbol, because it is right there where a great deal of the battle for a new world abides.

Colonialism that is not past, it is still present, still unfolding over the Blue Planet.

Thus, the word, the poetry and the Zen here wants to unfold bridges, wants to be a bridge, for the one that goes and for the ones that comes back.

Franz Fanon says *"Every colonized people- in other words, every people in whose soul an inferiority complex has been created by the death and burial of its local cultural originality- finds itself face to face with the language of the civilizing nation..."*

My aspiration is that it may be impossible to read this dreaming without the Latino reality and culture being evident.
Indo-Afro Latina, to be even more precise.

I aspire that the local cultural originality will be expressed here.
I call it walking Zen, the response to genocide and the oppression of the culture and the word as much as the Identity and the Memory.

Zen is expression, and expression is language.
And true language is not always words…

The language, when it becomes the language of the oppressor, becomes an alien language, and then there is no Zen.
In Zen as expression, as well as in poetry, muzik and words, the Culture, the Identity and the Memory do re-create the word, the rhythm and the meaning, and in this act of re-creating it opens the gates to meanings beyond the acceptable.

And there is a gate there, a horizon, a new and rebel Heart.

New feet for the walking, fresh and with no territory map, just as life and Love.

Just as true revolutions.

Creation and the Struggle are inseparable.

I find Zen there.
I find Love there.

Augusto Al Q'adi Alcalde

Río Ceballos, Córdoba, Argentina.
saludrebelde@yahoo.com.ar

Index

* Chopping down is nothing other than chopping down

* The Virtue of the Tao's Herb

* Bowl-Person

* The Moon

* Young Heart, Last kiss

* Night Brother's Zen (Ch'an) Way

The rat is time, the tiger is time

Augusto Al Q'adi Alcalde

Sesshin, Teisho, Day 5

Dogen Zenji, "The Time Being"

*"Look into this deeply. The hours of the day which are arrayed in the world now are
actualised by ascendance and descendance of the time being at each moment.
The rat is time, the tiger is time, sentient beings are time, Buddhas are time.
At this moment, you enlighten the entire world with three heads and eight arms.
You enlighten the entire world with the sixteen-foot golden body.
To fully actualise the entire world with the entire world is called thorough practice.
To fully actualise the golden body, to arouse the way-seeking mind, practise,
attain enlightenment and enter nirvana is nothing but time, nothing but being.*

*Just actualise. All time is all being. There is nothing extra.
A so-called extra being is completely an extra being.
Thus the time being half actualised is half of the time being completely actualised,
and a moment that seems to be missed is also completely being.
In the same way, even the moment before or after the moment that appears to be
missed is also complete in itself, the time being.
Vigorously abiding in each moment is the time being.
Do not mistakenly confuse it as non-being. Do not forcefully assert it as being.
You may suppose that time is only passing away
and not understand that time never arrives.*

*Although understanding itself is time,
understanding does not depend on its own arrival".*

Please sit comfortably, if you wish.
We continue today touching Dogen Zenji's teaching on Time Being.
It's my job to spoil the thing. The text is brilliant, clearly shining.

"Look into this deeply", he says.*"The hours of the day which are arrayed in the world now are actualised by ascendance and descendance of the time being at each moment"*
This is a very interesting point about the two aspects of practice, the two aspects of realisation itself. There comes to my mind one of Dogen's phrases where he says: *"When you practise Zen forward, know that each step is equal in substance"*.

So there is a process of going forward, walking forward, through the dharma path. No doubt about this. But for this to be real practice, we should really, intimately know, as Dogen says, that **each step is equal in substance**, each and every one of them.

Each zazen is equal in substance.
Each kiss to your lover, to your kids, equal in substance.
Each unique moment of our everyday life, the true Genjo Koan, equal in substance.

And that equality doesn't inspire and con-form only "our own" zazen; but each zazen, each moment of attention, act and zazen, are completely equal with Shakyamuni Buddha's zazen.
Awakened, unique, full and complete.

Just as our very life.

We should know that, says Dogen Zenji...
And he is talking about the aspect of **process** and the aspect of **substance**, which of course are not two and are perfectly inter-related, inter-walking.

Process and substance: **process** as our breathing and our life going forward into the unknown, as the unknown herself, practising, realising and fundamentally expressing this mist-erious Tao.

And **substance** when we take completely refuge this is to say abide, in this one heartbeat and step, this one moment, beyond continuity, beyond accumulation.

Just living, just dying, just loving, just inquiring, walking, dancing.

This is what this guy Dogen is saying here when he says *"time is actualised by ascendance and descendance of the time being at each moment"*
Not the horizontal chain of one step and **another** step, but the simple and single act of

our whole body-heart- mind ascending and descending into that substance line as "time being" itself, as attention itself, as actuality itself.

As the Genjo Koan, our very ordinary life.
Can we appreciate this?

There is a Korean Zen teacher called Chinul. He has a phrase I like to quote, a very simple phrase.　　　　　He says: *"Our practice is composed of sudden awakening and gradual personalisation"*.

Sudden awakening, sudden blooming, is what we are calling provisionally here *"equal in substance"*: each moment by moment shedding off body and mind.
And gradual personalisation is, of course, process: it takes time, takes putting to work our practice.

It is the coming forth of the shed off body-heart-mind. And this coming forth is a walking.

"Asking questions we walk", the Zapatista bros and sistahs do say...

"There the rat is time, the tiger is time, sentient beings are time, Buddhas are time", says our text.

And it continues, expressing: *"At this moment, you enlighten the entire world with three heads and eight arms. You enlighten the entire world with the sixteen-foot golden body."*

I find very interesting and crucial that here he is saying **not that you get "enlightened"**, you get awakened, but that **you enlighten the entire world**.
He says it twice. You enlighten the entire world **at this moment**.

So... how wide is that "you"?
As huge as a speck of dust, as small as the universe.

Shining Loving dancing and walking the new horizon as the true body and heart, the "new subjectivity-sociability that is so badly needed to revolutionize this wounded Mother Earth and all beings in all times and places.
This is truly "practice-play", this is truly realization, and this is truly Zen maturity as expression.

And this is not, of course, *"the self advances and confirms the ten thousand beings"*. It is not that we ourselves go out, taking on our shoulders the task of enlightening the world. Not like this.

It is what Dogen calls *"when actualised by the ten thousand beings, your body-and-mind as well as bodies and minds of others, drop away"*.

So there our practice is not only concerned with dropping away, shedding off, our own body and mind, but also **seeing intimately that in the same moment, bodies and minds of "others" are shed off too**.
Thus **we** enlighten the entire world.

Thus in **our** practice we do not merely search for our own enlightenment, our own awakening, our own perfection or change. What a huge illusion if so!!!

What **we** really wake up is the heart and walking of the bodhisattva, and at this very moment **we** enlighten, awaken the entire world.
"You enlighten it with three heads and eight arms and with the sixteen-foot golden body".
These are terms that reflect aspects of practice, faces of our own zazen as life.

Three heads and eight arms: this is pointing to those dharma guardians that sometimes we can see at the doors of Japanese or Chinese Zen centres. These are **the deities of passion**, like Fudo or Mahakala.
They have a fierce appearance, sometimes surrounded by fire, flames all around, maybe with a sword to cut off your head, one fang going up, two eyes crossed.
These deities we call the guardians of the dharma, of the Tao, and **they express the passion of life**, the practice-play-expression in the midst of the realm of the ten thousand grasses of delusion, of gaining and losing, of living, of dying.

We enlighten the entire world with that spirit, with that passion, this vital passion.

And also you enlighten the entire world at the same moment with the sixteen-foot golden body, which points the Buddha of limitless life.

*"To fully actualise the entire world **with the entire world** is called thorough, true practice."*
*"Fully **actualise the world with the world**"*: there we are not even doing anything!!!

The entire world enlightens the entire world, and we share that in our life.
It is our very life and walking.

"There no trace of realisation remains and this no-trace continues endlessly", says Dogen in the *Genjo Koan*. There we take an ocean and pour it into an ocean.
We take a mountain and pour it into a mountain.
We take the Genjo Koan and pour it into our ordinary and pregnant life, zazen into zazen, life into life, walking into walking...

"To fully actualise the golden body, to make the way-seeking mind come forth, practise, attain enlightenment and enter nirvana is nothing but being, nothing but time", Dogen completes the phrase. *"Just actualise all time as all being. There is nothing extra".*

Just actualise: **just make it actual**, real, with no memories, no ideas, just be completely open to the living fact. And when i say here "Just make" i mean "express it". "It" is already here.

There Mumon Zenji elsewhere in the *Mumonkan* says: *"Just one nen",* (that is, one moment of the mind completely in the now) *"just one nen sees through eternity. Time-lessness is in the now. When you see through this nen you see through the one who sees."*

Like this we actualise the sixteen-foot golden body and the entire world enlightens the entire world. Nothing lacking, full and complete, just like any moment in our daily life.

Can we appreciate this?

We do when we do respect this shining living fact.
Response-ability, the ability to respond and not merely react, abides there.

"There is nothing extra there", says Dogen Zenji, touching again and again the aspect of Sambhogakaya practice-play, full and complete, joyfully dancing, the quality of life, the quality of our very life, the true Genjo Koan.
Nothing extra.

To truly see this makes joy arise; and when joy arises, wonder comes together, and wonder is another word for deep Samadhi, **fascination with this mystery, complete fascination with the fact of empty oneness**.
Nothing extra.

It is at this point that Dogen Zenji, elsewhere in one of his poems, expresses: *"Inside the treasury of the dharma eye, a single grain of dust"*. If there were not that single grain of dust, truly it wouldn't be the treasury of the dharma eye!!!

Nothing extra, nothing lacking.
Just like we all here sharing and actualizing this living moment.

"A so-called extra being is thoroughly an extra being. Thus the time being half actualised is half of the time being completely actualised. And a moment that seems to be missed is also completely being."
A most interesting phrase: *"A moment that seems to be missed is also completely being"*.

So let us miss ourselves into this moment.

Miss yourself into this body-heart, into this Genjo Koan; because even when our body-heart-mind may think we are "missing" a moment, missing an opportunity, the dharma body, the body of the Tao herself keeps practice-play alive at some place, and you will find at certain mist-erious moments that It comes forth as the very Amitabha, the Buddha of endless, beginningless life, which is of course our own true and ordinary life.

Our text continues, saying: *"Vigorously abiding in each moment is the time being"*. *"Vigorously abiding in each moment"*: really, no comment is necessary for this phrase!!!

But we can say **abiding is finding our home**, finding our true place in and as this moment. There we stop wandering around, and we engage fully life, body and mind-heart into and as this moment.

Of course, "vigorously" here means "**no effort**", means "no direction", means "no con-trolling". That is the way in which we can have enough energy, enough vitality, **enough passion** to vigorously abide in this moment.

There we engage the totality of our human body, of which Dogen says *"It is the bones and marrows of the realm beyond consciousness and not consciousness"*.

So let us know that practice-play, realisation, expression, attention, zazen and our ordinary life is that: "bones and marrows of the realm beyond consciousness and not consciousness".

"Do not mistakenly confuse it as non-being", he says. *"Do not forcefully assert it as being. You may suppose that time is only passing away, and not understand that time never arrives."*
Very interesting. *"Time never arrives"*: so **there is no gap**.
As time does not arrive, we don't go away.

As attention does not arrive, zazen does not go away.
As realization does not arrive, our ordinary life does not go away.

Just the walking in joy of the Genjo Koan, our true Heart.

"Although understanding itself is time, understanding does not depend on its own arrival." Understanding does not depend at all on its own arrival: see, **its own arrival is happening at every moment**, every bit of the actual moment is itself understanding, is our body-heart, our walking, as understanding, each Koan, each heartbeat, each breath, each shikantaza, each zazen, each step in kinhin, under-standing itself.

And he is talking about understanding here, and I think there is a subtle difference between knowledge and know**ing**, understand**ing**, learn**ing**: that is a process.

Knowledge is just the ashes of the past.

It may be warm, but not burning.

Knowing, **understanding is a dynamic process of seeing things intimately with our body and heart-mind**, understanding them and letting them express and go.
In that way, we can **walk the dharma way lightly**.

And after all, as a known writer whose name i forgot said: *"The reason why angels can fly is that they take themselves so lightly"*.

Lightly: without the weight of expectations or memories, moment by moment understanding, learning the way.   "Lightly", this is with utter seriousness, just like a child playing.

"Understanding does not depend on its own arrival", he says here.

So we don't need to wait for its arrival. It is right here, right now.

Elsewhere, in a comment about the bodhisattva vows, Dogen Zenji says: *"The dharma wheel turns from the beginning. There is neither surplus nor lack. The whole universe is moistened with nectar, and the dharma is ready to harvest."*

The dharma, our very life, is ready to harvest.
It is harvest itself.
No farmer there, just the wind in the seed.
What is that?

There is a poem that says:

> *"Even in the dew*
> *on the tiny blade of some nameless grass,*
> *the moon*
> *is showing herself"*.

The moon is showing itself, vividly clear.
Let us settle there.

Cheers to that nameless grass!!!

By the way, what is your name?

Vitalising birth-and-death

Augusto Al Q'adi Alcalde

Teisho, Day 1

Zenki: "Undivided Activity" by Dogen Zenji (from the *Shobogenzo*), Section 1

"The great way of all Buddhas, thoroughly practised, is emancipation and realisation.
"Emancipation" means that in birth you are emancipated from birth,
in death you are emancipated from death.
Thus, there is detachment from birth-and-death and pervading birth-and-death.
Such is the complete practice of the great way.

There is letting go of birth-and-death and vitalising birth-and-death.
Such is the thorough practice of the great way.
"Realisation" is birth, birth is realisation.

At the time of realisation, there is nothing but birth totally actualised,
nothing but death totally actualised."

Please sit comfortably, if you wish.

This is our first day of Sesshin.
Usually they say it's the difficult day, in which the body is adjusting itself.
We're still not settled down into the schedule, flowing with the Rhythm.

And this may be so. But I think there is a certain beauty and subtle quality of the first day that is important for practice. The same quality of the first zazen we have ever done, or the first time we opened our eyes, the first time we did touch something...

A quality of innocence, of meeting the new, of meeting the fresh, the unknown.
I feel that is essential and important.

So let us emphasise that quality of the first day: not difficult, not easy, but just fresh, moment by moment, starting once and again our Sesshin.

Today we take up one of Dogen Zenji's chapters of the *Shobogenzo*, that can be translated as "Undivided Activity".

The Japanese word is "zenki", and has many possible translations.
"Undivided activity" is one of them.
Another possibility is "total experience".

And of course, as Dogen does through the entire *Shobogenzo*, it is pointing to practice, it is pointing to realisation, practice as realisation itself. Everyday life as realization itself.

The text begins, saying, *The great way of all buddhas, thoroughly practised, is emancipation and realisation*. "The great way", it says here.
"Way" is "do" or "Tao", also.

And if we go to that early poem by Lao Tzu, the *Tao Te Ching*, he says there that in front of that Tao, facing that Tao, we can point to it in two ways.
One is **the quality of the nameless**, the quality of the **unknown**, the Tao, the way without name, that **can't be known**.
And the other one is the Tao that can be named, the way that can be spoken of.

Lao Tzu there says, "If I must give it a name, I will call it Great".
We have here Dogen saying **the great way** of all Buddhas is emancipation and *realisation*.
"Way" is practice.

We call it zazen, but really it has no name, it has no place, and it has no actor, even though we can use a name.

When we use a name, we call it "shikantaza".

That is a Japanese word with Chinese roots that specifically means "just sitting", as it is widely translated: just sitting.
But it has another ideograph there that usually no-one seems to focus on.

"Shikan" is "just", and "za" is the same as in "zazen", "sitting".

But there is that interesting ideograph "**ta**", that means "hitting the centre, touching the core, touching the centre".

So maybe we also can drop the word "za" for "sitting", because there is no need to say "just sitting", **just**! is enough, moment by moment, step by step.

Just sitting, just breathing, just this step in kinhin.

Just this heartbeat in life.

That ideograph "ta", of "touching the centre", puts a real quality into the practice of shikantaza, and thus we can distinguish "just sitting" from "mere sitting".

We're talking here about **just** sitting, and in this very act, touching the heart of hearts, touching that centre that has no name, has no place, has no actor.

When we say "shikantaza" or we say "zazen", we also see three steps in that zazen: sit the body, sit the breath, and sit the mind-heart.

Let the body sit, let the breath sit, and let the heart, let the mind sit.

If the practice is just sitting and touching the source, to sit the body is full attention, full openness to **just the body** doing the practice, just **this** posture, just **this** step in kinhin, just **this** act when we are eating or resting.

And in everyday life, our true Genjo Koan, please do not take next moment for granted. Just this moment, full and complete, touching the marrow of joy.

And the same of course can be said about breath and mind-heart: just the breathing, just the mind, just the heart.

At that point we can drop this phrase about "three steps" in that practice: just the body, just the breathing, just the mind, they are not even one, in and as the single and passionate act of our whole being.
And please note i said **"our"**. It is our common and true body expressing the tao with no stink, just as a simple act in our simple daily life.
This is zazen, and this is what we call shikantaza practice and expression.

Dogen says here, *The great way of all Buddhas, thoroughly practised, is emancipation and realisation.*

"Thoroughly practised" is what he says with the ideographs "Zenki": true practice as undivided activity, as total, passionate experience.
But this is just one way of translating it.
"Zen" here is written in a different way from the "Zen" of "zazen" or "Zen way".

"Zen" here is written to mean **"entire, whole"** and also **"together"**.
And "ki" of "activity" also means **"possibility"**, **"capacity"** and **"response"**.

So that true practice, that undivided activity, is also the whole possibility, the whole capacity, **together** responding to the moment and life.

So here, when we are talking about practice we are talking about zazen and thus we are talking about life, everyday life, the Genjo Koan: that kind of practice is sitting, walking, breathing completely **intimate** with that no-name, that no-place, that no-actor, **as** that no-name and no-place herself.

There we touch the heart of "zenki", undivided activity, and it comes forth as ourselves, as the body of the Buddha, this is the "Body of Awaken-ing", as limitless life herself.

The great way of the Buddhas, says Dogen, *is emancipation and realisation.*

And he continues saying, *"Emancipation" means that in birth you are emancipated from birth, in death you are emancipated from death. Thus, there is detachment from birth-and-death and pervading birth-and death. Such is the complete practice of the great way. There is letting go of birth-and-death and vitalising birth-and-death. Such is the true practice of the great way.*
He talks about emancipation and also some qualities of that emancipation: detachment, pervading, letting go and **vitalising**.
When we talk about emancipation, the natural question is: "Who or What is holding us?"
And if we go deep into our hearts, we will find that truly nothing or no-one is holding us, even though that sense of emancipation doesn't come forth.

And that is where we touch that sign of life that in the Buddhayana we call "Dukkha".

There are many ways of translating "Dukkha". The usual one is "suffering" or "anguish". And this is certainly one possibility.
And this is the "Dukkha" that we talk about being transcended, the need to transcend that "Dukkha", that suffering or that anguish. And the whole of the Buddhayana is about that.

But there is another translation for that word "Dukkha" which is also useful.
And the translation is "**un-satisfaction**".

When Dukkha comes as "un-satisfaction", this can be the fire, the passion and the power that makes us go forward, to walk the Utopia.

This is the Zen mind of "not enough".

Any moment, any step, any realisation, we are not enough. One more step!

Thus that "Dukkha" as un-satisfaction can lead us to realise these qualities of detachment, pervading, letting go and vitalising that Dogen is talking about here.

When he says "**detachment**", I feel he is saying: "Be completely one with the Tathagata, with this coming forth as it is". This is truly detachment.

And then we touch the characteristic of **pervading** that belongs to this emancipation.

It's not just being completely one with the Tathagata as it comes, but also not even one, **as** the Tathagata, as this very life coming forth moment by moment.

The other two characteristics are crucial to Zen practice: **letting go and vitalising**.
"Letting go" is what is said in Soto practice, following Dogen's advice: dropping off, shedding off, body-and-mind.
That is to sit in that place that is no-place, no-name, completely unknown, shedding off body-and-mind.
And when that happens, the other aspect of vitality, "**vitalis-ing**", comes forth naturally.

Call it Love if you wish...

There, abiding nowhere, the mind comes forth, the body comes forth, freeing the many beings, the shed off body-and-mind dancing and shining as the true heart, true body, as the mountains, as the rivers, as the horizon, as the many beings, as "us".

Dogen Zenji continues, saying, *"Realisation" is birth, birth is realisation. At the time of realisation there is nothing but birth totally actualised, nothing but death totally actualised. "Realisation" is birth,* says the old teacher, here. That is to say, realisation is the coming forth, realisation is that act of coming forth.

It has many forms.
In our tradition of Buddhayana, we talk about the Buddha, the "Awaken-ing", sitting under the bodhi tree and the star coming forth to confirm, actualize him as the Awakened One.

This is one coming forth: the star, the many beings, any sound, any feeling, any thing, coming forth and touching us intimately and deeply.

That is the realisation of the Awakened heart itself.
And there is truly hope for a new world there.

But there is another one which I think can be even more important, and that is the coming forth of the Buddha from under the bodhi tree, the coming forth of practice as expression into the world, for the many beings.

"Realisation" is birth, is that coming forth, says Dogen, *totally actualised,* heart, body, breath, mind, becoming actual, moment by moment, with full attention, in total openness.
Thus we can live zazen and our life as "zenki", undivided activity, as total experience, realising as birth itself the whole possibility, the entire capacity and passion of our practice as this very living moment.

We said before that in translating the word "zenki" we have also the meanings of "together" and "response". I think these two words are two deep archetypes for practice and life itself: "together" and "response".

Dogen says it over and over: *"The ten thousand beings advance and actualise the self, and this is called awakening".*
We can also say this is called practice, endless practice, called life, endless life.

This is called joy, this is called dancing.
With that practice, that joy, that dancing, that Love completely intimate with the undivided activity of this very moment, each zazen, each step, each breath, each moment in our very daily life is the total capacity, the whole possibility that we call "zenki".

And also, and most important, the "**together response**" of the ten thousand beings advancing and actualising the self.
Not as some abstract entity, but this very body, heart and mind, this very and only moment in our common life.

Let's drop the concept of "self".
Let's drop the concept of "many beings", let's drop the concept of one who drops them.

Our story today says:

"Their son was baptized on the coast.

The baptism taught him what was sacred.

They gave him a sea shell:"So you will learn to love the water."

They opened a cage and let the bird go free: "So you will learn to love the air."

They gave him a geranium: "So you will learn to love the earth."

And they gave him a little bottle sealed up tight: "Don't ever, ever open it.

So you will learn to love Mystery."

A black brother in Hawaii, a drummer from Africa, said to me once at a very ripe moment: "We cannot hold the past. We don't have the future. We only have the great shining gift of this moment. It is a gift, and that's why it is called "the present".

True indeed!

Cheers!!!

Let us settle there.

Birth in its immediacy

Augusto Al Q'adi Alcalde

Teisho 2

Zenki: Undivided Activity, by Dogen Zenji (from the *Shobogenzo*), Sections 1, 2, 3 and 4

> *"At the time of realisation there is nothing but birth totally actualised,*
> *nothing but death totally actualised.*
> *Such activity makes birth wholly birth, death wholly death.*
> *Actualised just so at this moment, this activity is neither large nor small,*
> *neither remote nor urgent.*
> *Birth in its right-now-ness is undivided activity.*
> *Undivided activity is birth in its immediacy.*
>
> *Birth neither comes nor goes. Birth neither appears nor is already existing.*
> *Thus, birth is totally manifested, death is totally manifested.*
>
> *Know that there are innumerable beings in yourself.*
>
> *Also there is birth, and there is death.*
>
>
> *Quietly see whether birth and all things that come together with birth*
> *are inseparable or not. There is neither a moment nor a thing that is apart from birth.*
> *There is neither an object nor a mind that is apart from birth."*

Sit comfortably, if you need it.

Well, this is our second full day of Sesshin, and some of you are leaving today or tomorrow. Please don't be concerned with that.
Until the moment of leaving comes, you are here.

So **please be here**, even if this is your last day, completely here, one day's Sesshin.

Forget everything about time apparently running away.
Time doesn't run away, it doesn't come.

It's just here.

That is the context and quality of our zazen and of our life.

The day that you live, tomorrow, today, seven days from now, one hundred years, we are always **here**, and this is the place, and this is the realisation of Zen practice and it's expression in daily life..

Today we continue with the chapter "Undivided Activity" from the *Shobogenzo* by Dogen Zenji. He says today, *at the time of realisation, there is nothing but birth totally actualised, nothing but death totally actualised. Such activity makes birth truly birth, death truly death.*

Dogen Zenji likes to play with words and ideographs, metaphors and poetry, as if he were speaking "Dogenese".
And in that sense he uses many of them to point to the same thing.

Here, birth is the subject of this essay, and from that he is pointing to the basic fact of Zen practice, what is called realisation, birth, coming forth, life.
By realisation we mean "seeing into true nature", as Bodhidharma says. **Seeing** into true nature. But it's not only **seeing into** true nature, but **seeing as** true nature herself.
And that seeing is not only encapsulated with the eyes.
It's our whole body's living experience of true nature, as our self, as the world itself.
As we said before, true "physicality".
We say that Zen begins there, with that seeing into true nature.

And thus we talk about the so-called Three Bodies of the Buddha, which point to that same seeing from different angles.
We say the Dharmakaya is the Body of Emptiness; the Sambhogakaya is the Body of Fullness and Joy; and the Nirmanakaya is the Body of Uniqueness.

So realisation or birth in this context is seeing, expressing and personalising these Three Bodies: potent creative emptiness, fullness and completeness in joy that is the Sambhogakaya, and the uniqueness of each being, of each moment, each life.

Dogen continues, saying, *Such activity makes birth totally birth, death totally death. Actualised just so at this moment, this activity is neither large nor small.*
He is saying here that this activity which he calls birth or undivided activity is actualised just so at this moment.
So there is no need for us to **do** something for that to be actualised!!! It is being actualised, moment by moment, as the Three Bodies of the Buddha.

Just so at this moment, says Dogen Zenji.

This is what is happening already, so our practice is to join the dance of this unique, living moment, dive into actuality so that we ourselves disappear and the undivided activity of life is our true home.
This activity, this undivided, total activity, says Dogen, *is neither large nor small*, neither comes nor goes.

So this is just one Koan as total activity, just one moment of attention, one breath fully engaging body-heart-and-mind, and the body of actuality and the mind of the mountains, oceans and the many beings, beyond concepts of "large", "small", "remote" or "near".

At that point, **this** point, this practice is itself undivided activity, whole body-heart-and-mind activity, burning completely into the present, the gift, the Tathagata, "that which thus comes and thus goes".

Our text continues, saying, *Birth in its right-now-ness is undivided activity. Birth in its right-now-ness.*
"Right-now-ness", what a good name for the nameless; and, as Dogen says, practice **is** realisation itself.
It is also a good name for practice itself, for life itself: "birth in its right-now-ness".

What Dogen is saying here is, birth or life or realisation, in its intimate quality of right-now-ness, is practice, is realisation, is zazen as undivided, total activity; is daily life as total experience with the ten thousand beings, **as** a single sound, a single thought, a single breath, a single step in our kinhin, coming forth and actualising the self.

Deep into the heart of life, deep into that birth, Buddha-nature comes forth in its right-now-ness. Let us settle there our zazen, our Genjo Koan-our very life, our shikantaza.

Beyond "inner" or "outer", "me" or "others", "good" or "bad", "before" or "after".
Just **this**, just filling the whole universe as our true body, our true home.

Dogen says that birth and that complete activity neither comes nor goes, nor appears nor is already existing.
So the moment of realisation never comes; the moment of ignorance never goes away.

Realisation itself never goes away, and ignorance never comes.

Thus there is no place for concepts, no place for any aiming, no place for any map, because there is no territory; and certainly no place for any "technique" in zazen.

Just body, breath and heart-mind as one, in deep intimacy, sitting, breathing...
Walking as that no-place itself, full of creation, nothing lacking, and preciously unique...

Our text continues, saying; *Know that there are innumerable beings in yourself.*
That's a very interesting phrase.

Sometimes we think there is only Jekyll and Mr Hyde, but here Dogen is saying **there are innumerable beings in yourself.** And not only that: there are innumerable beings **as** yourself, not merely inhabiting under our skin, but as the whole of life, the whole beings, past, present, future, all times and all spaceⅭengaging in zazen **as** our self, **as** our true body.
Dogen says, *also there is birth, and there is death. Quietly see whether birth and all things that come together with birth are inseparable or not.*
See if birth and things that arise together with birth are one or not, Dogen Zenji is saying here.

We want to push away ignorance and keep wisdom; we want to push away death and keep life; we want to push away distraction and keep attention, in our life and practice.
But all comes together.
And as the Muslims bros and sistahs say, "One can't jump out of his own shadow".

So the body is practice, and the body is realisation.
And also the shadow is practice, and the shadow is realisation.
We can though be a tree, and the shadow became a shade.

Our "walking words" story today says:

"Everything has, we all have, a face and a mark.
Dogs and snakes and sea gulls, you and i, those who are living and those who have
already lived, and all who walk, wriggle, or fly: we all have a face and a mark.

That's what the Mayas believe.

And they believe that the mark, the invisible mark, is more of a face than the visible face.

By your mark you'll be known..."

And thus we meet the other meaning of "Zenki", "undivided activity".
Ignorance, death, distraction, wisdom, life, body, shadow, attention, **intimate as
"together response"**.
That is the other meaning of "total action": "together response", completely available
for the star to come forth and wake up the Awakened.

Completely available for the coming forth from under the Bodhi tree and to engage and
involve in the practice for the many beings.

There is a poem that says:

> "All night long, I've chanted all the Buddha names,
> All of which were once my original name".

In the shining right-now-ness of zazen and life, let us settle into that original name.
We don't need to search around.

"Right now" neither comes nor goes, appears nor is already existing.

Just listen, listen.

The singing in the rain is blowing in the wind.

Want to share?

Just like riding in a boat

Augusto Al Q'adi Alcalde

Sesshin, Teisho Day 3

Zenki (Undivided Activity) by Dogen Zenji
From the *Shobogenzo*, Section 5

> *"Birth is just like riding in a boat.*
> *You raise the sails and row with the oar.*
> *Although you row, the boat gives you a ride and without the boat no-one could ride.*
> *But you ride in the boat and your riding makes the boat what it is.*
> *Investigate a moment such as this.*
>
> *At just such a moment, there is nothing but the world of the boat.*
> *The sky, the water and the shore all are the boat's world,*
> *which is not the same as a world that is not the boat's.*
>
> *When you ride in a boat, your body-and-mind and the environs together*
> *are the undivided activity of the boat.*
> *The entire earth and the entire sky are both the undivided activity of the boat.*
> *Thus birth is nothing but you; you are nothing but birth."*

Sit comfortably, if you need it.

Today is our third full day of Sesshin.

Traditionally, we say the third day is the turning day, the turning point in which our Sesshin turns around. But I used to say, during the years of doing Sesshin I found that if a seven-day Sesshin is happening, the third day is the turning day; if a three-day Sesshin is happening, the first day is the turning day!!!

34

So something happens there that makes things change, which is not really related with time. Probably if we are doing a 30-day Sesshin, the 15th will be the turning point!

So something related with our own mind, our own attitude and perception of time is what makes a moment the turning point.

So we can say, yes, this is our third full day and is our turning point in Sesshin; but also take up the practice of actualizing every day, every zazen, every moment in daily life as the turning point of our Sesshin.

This is not something that we **have to make**; this is something that already is, and making it the turning point is diving completely into that wonderful possibility.

There we touch what Dogen Zenji is calling here "undivided activity" or "whole activity", or "activity of the whole" itself.

He says today in the text, *Birth is just like riding in a boat*. Birth is just like riding on a boat. By "birth", here, we are meaning the Tathagata, which is a word that the Buddha used to refer to himself.

Tathagata means "that which thus comes and thus goes".

So that Tathagata is itself the coming forth, and it is birth, which *is just like riding in a boat*, as Dogen Zenji says.

In other parts of the *Shobogenzo*, he says, "Realisation has no beginning; practice has no end". Again he says, "Practice has no beginning and realisation has no end".
To settle and to personalise that fact is indeed riding the dharma boat.

So practice is just like riding on a boat; realisation is just like riding, beyond time, beyond space.

The boat here is the dharma, the Way, the Tao and of course being the dharma is our very own life. And that boat, as the Buddha says, has certain signs or characteristics.

He spoke about the three signs of life: Anicca, Anatta and Dukkha. "Anicca" means impermanence, means change. "Anatta" is "no separate self", no self that is not in together-ness with other selves.
And "Dukkha" is "un-satisfaction" or suffering.

These are the characteristics of the dharma boat, the life boat.
And it depends on how we relate with them what the quality of the boat and the quality of the riding will be.

So: birth and each moment, each spark of life, presenting clearly Aimpermanence@, presenting totally clearly "no separate entity", presenting totally clearly "un-satisfaction", as the form and quality of the boat.
And Dukkha happens when Anicca and Anatta are not really appreciated as great opportunities for dance and joy.

So we resist that, we resist that change, we resist that birth, thinking that we can just centre into ourselves, stay there, resisting that change.
But what happens is that this is obviously not possible!!!

And so the practice is to appreciate and take joy into that fact, that everything is changing, that there are innumerable beings in ourselves, and that we ourselves are intimately linked with all beings, all things in the so-called Three Times: present, past and future, throughout all space and time.

This is the riding of the boat.

And Dogen continues, saying, *Although you row, the boat gives you a ride*.
That rowing is practice.

And sometimes, deep practice takes the form of the "Don't-know" mind: deep zazen, deep Genjo Koan, deep shikantaza as "Don't-know".

Not just that "Don't-know" that is making time for finding out something, but just that pure "Don't-know" mind-heart.

This is the mind and heart of the mystery, zazen and our very life as the mystery itself, facing and expressing and walking intimately that mystery itself.

When Bodhidharma was asked by the Emperor Wu what was the first principle of the holy dharma, he said, *"Vast space and emptiness; nothing to be called holy"*.
That is very interesting.

Vast space and emptiness is then another name for our practice.

If we touch, receive, walk intimately that "Don't-know" mind-heart, we have endless, limitless space; endless, limitless potential, creative emptiness.

"Nothing to be called sacred", or "Nothing to be called holy", expresses and walks Bodhidharma there.
And that vast space, vast emptiness is quite an ordinary fact. Just as our daily life itself.
And "ordinary", in the ideograph that is written, also means "timeless".

So, as Dogen Zenji says in another chapter of his *Shobogenzo*, "*in the domain of brothers and sisters, drinking tea and eating rice is the vital activity of the Buddhas*".

So as long as we feel that Sesshin is "something special", that zazen is something special, that to be a Zen student or a Buddhist is something special, we are altogether missing the point.
The point here is an activity of our whole body-heart-and-mind that is completely ordinary.
"Nothing to be called holy" there, just as eating rice and having tea.

Dogen says that the transmission of the right way of drinking tea and having rice is the true dharma, the true Way, the true Tao.

So let our zazen and our walking the events of our Genjo Koan, our ordinary life itself, be as ordinary and tasty as drinking tea and having rice.

Dogen says, continuing the text, *Your riding makes the boat what it is*.
I find this is a very interesting phrase: *Your riding makes the boat what it is*.

Your practice-play makes the boat what it is. Same with life...

And regarding practice, he says, "*To study the Buddha-dharma is to study the self; to study the self is to forget the self; to forget the self is to be awakened by the ten thousand beings*".
That is the riding that makes the boat and our life the dharma, the Way and the Tao herself.

When the boat rides us, we have birth, we have practice and realisation.
Then the boat and the ten thousand beings advance and authenticate the self.

Thus at that moment the self is not encapsulated into our skin, but shines in all beings **as** all beings, as the very boat and the dharma itself.

Here *your riding makes the boat what it is*, and the Koan comes forth and authenticates our life; shikantaza, and that one sparky moment of full attention and openness, advances and actualises our self as the boat itself, filling the whole universe.

Just one breath, just one moment of attention, making the boat what it is.

"It is a dream", said Yamamoto Gempo Roshi.
That is another essential quality of the play and the practice.

That dream quality is intimate with what we call "makyo" in Zen, "mysterious vision". That quality of dreams comes forth when our zazen is altogether settled, we are completely open, we are completely into that attention that makes our common life unfold. Certainties fall away: "me" and "other", "inner" and "outer" fall away, "day" and "night" dualities also are shed off.
And there is a certain quality of dream, a certain quality that we call "makyo", mysterious vision, which Yasutani Roshi used to say is awakening itself.

Dogen continues, saying, *At just such a moment, there is nothing but the world of the boat.*
At just such a moment, no special moment.
This very moment!!!

Because *"when you see and hear things with your whole body-and-mind, you understand intimately"*.
When you see and hear things with your whole body-and-heart-mind, not just **this** whole body-and-mind, but the whole body-and-mind that is the actuality of the boat, life itself.
When we see and hear things with that body-and-mind, we *understand intimately.*
At such a moment: just the moment, we ourselves, as the living moment itself, completely intimate with zazen and life.

We say, in one of our sutras, "Nen nen ju shin ki, Nen ne fu ri shin". "Nen" is the **mind in the now**.
That attention-heart, is one with the Mind; that heart, does come forth from the Mind, says that sutra.

The mind in the now, just as this very moment.

At such a moment, *there is nothing but the world of the boat*, says Dogen.
This is all-inclusive zazen, all inclusive life, having joy and fullness in the world of the boat.
Full and complete, potent, creative **emptiness** as our own true nature and heart; the **fullness** and completeness of each being, each moment and ourselves just as we are; and the **uniqueness** of each breath, each zazen.

Each step fully engaging body-and-heart-mind, fully engaging space, mountains, oceans and the many beings, the whole world of the dharma, the whole world of our very common life, **as** this zazen, this one breath, this step, this boat, this Genjo Koan, our daily life itself.

When you ride in a boat, body-and-mind and the environs together are the undivided activity of the boat, says Dogen here.
"Together" is extra: not one, one two, not me, not others; just the undivided, total, whole capacity and response of the dharma boat, coming to birth moment by moment as the unborn, unknown mystery, just as our zazen and life itself.

This chapter ends saying, *Birth is nothing but you; you are nothing but birth*, birth being practice, realisation itself.
Birth is nothing but you, so let birth advance and become our true nature.
You are nothing but birth, he says after this.

So let's drop even that "true nature" away, so that only practice, only realisation, only our very life, only the dharma boat rides this living moment.

Our Latino Land story today says:

The light of dead stars travels
And by the flight of their splendour they are alive.
The guitar, which does not forget its companion, makes music without any hand.
The voice travels on, leaving the mouth behind.

And let's appreciate this, the whole activity of the boat.

Cheers!!!

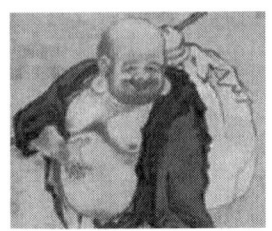

Birth does not hinder death, death does not hinder birth...

Augusto Al Q'adi Alcalde
Sesshin, Teisho Day 4

Zenki (Undivided Activity) by Dogen Zenji
From the *Shobogenzo*, Section 6

"Zen Master Yuan Wu said, 'birth is undivided activity, death is undivided activity'
Clarify and investigate these words.
What you should investigate is: While the undivided activity of birth has no beginning
or end and covers the entire earth and the entire sky,
it hinders neither birth's undivided activity nor death's undivided activity.
At the moment of death's undivided activity, while it covers the entire earth and the
Entire sky, it hinders neither death's undivided activity nor birth's undivided activity.

This being so, birth does not hinder death; death does not hinder birth."

Please sit comfortably, if you wish.

Today we keep going through the *Shobogenzo* chapter on "Undivided (or total) Activity", by Dogen.

He is, throughout the whole chapter, taking these terms "birth", "death" and "undivided activity" and playing with them, with all the possible relationships between those aspects of our own life and practice.

Here he is quoting Master Yuan Wu saying *"Birth is undivided activity. Death is undivided activity."* And then he says that we should *clarify and investigate these* **words**, "undivided activity".
In the context of practice, "undivided" or "whole" or "together" is what elsewhere Dogen expresses as *"fully engaging body-and-mind, we understand things intimately"*.

So this "undivided" has the quality of fully engaging body-and-mind-heart, but also **the quality of intimacy**: *"you Aunderstand intimately"*.
That intimacy is beyond "one", beyond "two".

It's hard to have "communication": the Koan practising the Koan, shikantaza practising shikantaza, Sesshin doing Sesshin by itself, no Sangha neither Zen student to be found there.

This undivided activity is also taken up in other chapters of the *Shobogenzo* where Dogen talks about "all-inclusive study", "all-inclusive practice", "all-inclusive realisation".
That is, all-inclusive breath, all-inclusive step in kinhin and everyday life.
Un-divided activity.

That word "activity" is very interesting, and we think we understand easily what that means. But if we go to a subtle point, we find that activity, or the act of zazen, the act of being alive, the act of forgetting the self in zazen, refers to that activity not as the usual or conditioned or mechanical activity of observing, watching, labelling, evaluating that now turns toward the so-called "inside", toward the so-called "internal", with the same attitude it has with the so-called "external".

It's not like that, but a totally new, totally fresh, fearless, total vision engaging our whole body-heart-and-mind and the heart of life **as** this very living moment, "**together**", as Dogen Zenji says.

Together as the Genjo Koan, as zazen, as shikantaza itself, diving intimately into peace, dignity freedom and respect.

That is attention and openness, and the essence of all movement, all action, all undivided activity, indeed of all life that deserves this name.

Clarify* and *investigate* these *words, says Dogen Zenji.

What you should investigate is: While the undivided activity of birth has no beginning or end and covers the entire earth and the entire sky. **That** *has no beginning nor end and covers the entire earth and the entire sky*, says Dogen Zenji there.
That is beyond time.

We tend to think of "beginning" as before, "birth" before and "death" there in the future. But here he is saying: no beginning, no end.

Actually no birth, no death.
Beyond time.

"Zazen is to study the self", says Dogen Zenji.
"To study the self is to forget the self."

That **act** of forget-ing the self does not come from the memory, does not come from any comparison from the past. Neither does it from any "decision".
The moment, a sound, a Koan (as inquiring body-heart-mind), zazen, life, advances and actualises itself as the self itself.

So **this** is "beyond time".
This **free activity** is beyond time, not influenced by knowledge from the past; and also not projecting to an ideal future that we may call realisation.

Dogen says in another essay called "Being-Time": *"Each moment is all beings. Each moment is the entire world. No being or any world is left out of the present moment."*

There we touch again this all-inclusive practice and life that can truly be called "undivided activity".
"No being or any world is left out of the present moment."
That is the context of our practice, and that is the true body-heart that expresses zazen and Zen in everyday life, our true Genjo Koan.

He continues, saying, *It covers the entire earth and the entire sky.*

That practice, that realisation and life activity-expression that we call zazen or Zen **as** the whole earth, **as** the whole sky.
Covering completely earth and sky, body, heart-mind, breath and environs, **as** earth, as sky itself.

No person to be found there.
Just this sky, this earth, this moment, this very life, forget-ing the self in the simple act of zazen.
The simple and whole act of being alive.

Here zazen is, as Dogen says in one of his poems:

> *"A snowy heron on the snowfield*
> *where winter grass is unseen*
> *Hides itself in its own figure."*

"Hides itself in its own figure": that is a wonderful and powerful inspiring metaphor for our life and practice.

Dogen says also, *It hinders neither death's undivided activity nor birth's undivided activity.*
Here we have another teaching about practice.

Life and practice as the healing art of expressing Buddha-nature. This is to say the Awaken-ing Nature.
It hinders neither birth's nor death's undivided activity.
Hiding itself in its own figure it does not hinder birth, does not hinder death.

This is shikantaza and everyday life as the simple, innocent, humble act of intimacy with true nature, shining and dancing all over the earth.
At this very living moment and heart it hinders neither birth's nor death's undivided activity.
It doesn't hinder the coming forth of the Tathagata which is healing and inspiration itself.

Here we find zazen with the beauty and passion of the ten thousand beings advancing from the source to the source, as the very source itself, body-and-mind-heart blooming in a moment-to-moment attention, inquiring and flowing with no purpose, no expectations and also no postponing.
No postponing, as the right-now-ness of birth that we call practice, we call realisationwe call everyday life, we call the Genjo Koan.

Can we appreciate this?

The text ends, saying, *This being so, birth does not hinder death; death does not hinder birth*. Birth does not hinder death; death does not hinder birth!

Keizan Zenji, in one of the poems of the *Denko-roku*, says:

> *"Though clear waters extend to the vast blue sky*
> *How can it compare with the hazy moon on a spring night?*
> *Most people want to have it pure white,*
> *But sweep as you will, you cannot empty the mind."*

Clear enough, huh? Cheers!!!

The entire earth
and the entire sky appear

Augusto Al Q'adi Alcalde
Sesshin, Teisho day 5

Zenki (Undivided Activity) by Dogen Zenji (from the *Shobogenzo*), Section 7

"Both the entire earth and the entire sky appear in birth as well as in death.
However, it is not that one and the same entire earth and sky
are fully manifested in birth
and also fully manifested in death: although not one, not different;
although not different, not the same; although not the same, not many.

Similarly, in birth there is undivided activity of all things,
and in death there is undivided activity of all things.
There is undivided activity in what is not birth and not death.

There is birth and there is death in undivided activity."

Sit comfortably, if you wish.
Dogen says today, *Both the entire earth and the entire sky appear in birth as well as in death.*
What is it, this entire earth?
What is it, that entire sky?
And what is the nature of that "appear"?

All this has to do with our practice. All this has to do with our life.
The entire earth, says Dogen. This is zazen as "just form".

The entire earth, mountains, rivers, the many beings appear as **the undivided physicality** of shikantaza, the **solidity** of the Koan, the **total response** of zazen, intimately one with the life of the earth itself.
The entire earth appears.
Thus the entire earth comes forth, as a mountain of attention, as our true blood and body.

Both the entire earth and the entire sky appear in birth as well as in death.
The entire sky: zazen as "just space", vital space, fearless space, with no beginning, no end; no front, no back; no depth and no height.

Space beyond concepts appears, moment by moment appears, as "Zenki", the whole possibility and capacity of shikantaza, the entire capacity of the Genjo Koan, our very life itself, **the together response** of zazen, intimately one with the wonder and freedom of the unknown.
The energy and the pulse of Amitabha, limitless life.

The entire sky appears: this energy and wisdom without any conflict, with no direction, no option or effort.
Thus the entire sky appears, coming forth as total freedom, as our true heart and mind.

The entire earth and the entire sky appear in birth as well as in death, says our text. "Appear", moment by moment appear. **So please look!**

Where does this earth and this sky not shine?

This is the coming forth, the Tathagata as our blood and body, heart and mind, coming forth everywhere as earth, as sky, as zazen itself.
Here practice is intimate flowing with the coming forth, as the coming forth itself, the self totally forgotten.
So "just the coming forth" is our true home, our true heart, totally new and unexpected, leaving no memories or trace, the essence of all life in the Three Times, timeless life.

The entire earth and the entire sky appear in birth as well as in death.

Realization here is the dance of beauty, the power of innocence itself, as this very living moment, our bones, our marrow.

The text continues, saying, *Although not one, not different; although not different, not the same; although not the same, not many.*

That is quite interesting and subtle: not one, not different, not the same, not many!!! This is "appear" itself, vividly clear.

This is the true nature of the Buddha-Tao, the original face of the Genjo Koan, **the blooming and ordinary immensity** of our very life, of shikantaza.

Not one, not different, not the same, not many.

Each Koan, each act of shikantaza fully engaging body-and-mind, each moment in our everyday life, the **total response** of forget-ting the self in the act.

Not one, not different, that is clear.

Not the same, not many, this shines in that very act of forgetting the self in the Koan, in zazen, in shikantaza, in the real ground of the play, our very life itself.

It is not only that the white crane on the snowfield hides itself in its own figure. It is not only that the crane disappears and just the essential snowfield shines as the heart of true nature.

It is not just that we drop the crane, the snowfield and the act of hiding itself.

Not just that!

When we see with the same heart as the haiku poetess that wrote

> *"White crane on the snowfield:*
> *If it were not for her voice,*
> *it will go unnoticed"*

When we see as that heart, great life appears.

The universe is born and the simple act of taking a step frees the many beings as ourselves.

Dogen continues, saying, *similarly, in birth there is undivided activity of all things, and in death there is undivided activity of all things.*

This is the ordinary world, just as it is.
There is undivided activity: all beings, all things, in all space and all time, are totally immersed in birth and death, dancing that undivided activity.

Then he says, *There is undivided activity in what is not birth and not death*.
That's interesting: *in what is not birth and not death*.
This is the moment beyond time of dropping off body-and-mind, of forgetting the self.

Nothing there.
"**No-thing**" there.
No birth, no death.

The ground of inspiration and encouragement, with all hindrances of the mind falling away, disappearing.
As the *Heart Sutra* says, "No hindrance in the mind, therefore no fear".

Dogen continues, saying, *There is birth and there is death in undivided activity*.
*There **is** birth and there **is** death in undivided activity*.
Birth: the birth of deep Koan play, deep shikantaza, deep zazen, hiding itself in its own figure as the undivided activity of all beings, in all space and time itself.

There is death in undivided activity, says Dogen here.
Death: "If it were not for its voice, it will go unnoticed".

If it were not for its voice, that voice coming forth from the heart that is no-where-ness itself, giving life to the essential nature in the act of killing the snowfield and the crane, bringing them to limitless life **as** that voice itself. That intimate voice of the heart-mind of zazen, as the Buddha-Tao itself, our true body, our true mind, our true life.

Someone told me that in Spain, they paid respect to an Arab tower that was destroyed. They did not reconstruct the tower, evoking what once was there. In front of the big hole where that tower once was, a bronze child, sitting hugging his knees, looks deeply at it.

Let us settle our Koan, shikantaza and zazen, our life, as that primal innocence.

And in that deep look bring forth Maitreya, the Buddha-to-be-Born's tower, in which each being, each breath, each step, each moment is a jewel beyond any value.

I truly hope we can appreciate this.
Cheers!!!

Like someone asleep searching with his hand

Augusto Al Q'adi Alcalde
Sesshin, Teisho Day 6

Zenki (Undivided Activity) by Dogen Zenji (from the *Shobogenzo*), Sections 8 and 9

*"The undivided activity of birth and death is like a young person bending and
stretching his arm, or it is like someone asleep searching with his hand
behind his back for the pillow.
This is realisation in vast wonderful light.
About just such a moment you may suppose that because realisation is
manifested in undivided activity, there was no realisation prior to this.
However, before this realisation, undivided activity was manifested.
But undivided activity manifested previously
does not hinder the present realisation of undivided activity.
Because of this your understanding can be manifested moment after moment."*

Sit comfortably, if you wish.

We continue going through Dogen's "Undivided Activity", an essay of the
Shobogenzo. And today we reach the end of it, the end of the essay.
And it is also coincidentally our last Teisho of this Sesshin.

In moments such as this, in any Sesshin, usually one can begin to feel that time
is running out. We are approaching the end of the Sesshin.

And one possibility is, as time is running out, to get more and more anxious about doing something special before the Sesshin ends.

This attitude only leads to frustration.

If we press too much, with a preconceived idea of what the results of the Sesshin will be, this leads to frustration.

And also another kind of attitude can be present at moments such as this, and is that voice that says, "Well, I've been sitting here for six days and didn't reach something special and so what can I do, now we have one day ahead?

So throw it, you know: "I'll spend the time sitting the most comfortably possible until the last bell." This attitude also is no good. It doesn't take us to any place.

So it doesn't matter really if this is the last day of Sesshin, if this is our last zazen or if this is our last breath in life.

The thing is always the same, in Zen practice: beyond time, moment by moment, actualising our zazen; moment by moment, actualising our life, our Genjo Koan.

So the end of Sesshin may come, but it is useful in moments like this to make Sesshin finish right now!!!

Right now, finish it with this breath, this Koan, this shikantaza.

Complete Sesshin, finish Sesshin.

And next moment, next breath, next Koan, Sesshin starts again and finishes itself also in the same act.

This is basically what Dogen Zenji has been talking about during this Sesshin, in his essay "Undivided Activity": whole activity, complete activity, moment by moment, renewing itself.

He says today, *the undivided activity of birth and death is like a young person bending and stretching his arm, or it is like someone asleep searching with his hand behind his back for the pillow. This is realisation in vast and wonderful light.*

This is, after all we have said about undivided activity, after all, it's perfectly a simple and natural act, as a person reaching for the pillow in the night.

There is a Case in the *Hekigan Roku* in which Ungan asks Dogo, *"How does the bodhisattva Kanzeon use all these hands and eyes?"*
Dogo said, *"It is like a person in the middle of the night reaching behind his head for his pillow".*

Exactly the same point.
Ungan is asking, "What is the action of the bodhisattva of compassion helping and saving the many beings with all those many hands and eyes?"
Dogo says, "Quite natural: it is like a person in the middle of the night reaching behind his head for his pillow".

That quality of a perfectly natural act of our whole body and being is the essence of Love and compassion and the essence of the act of freeing, liberating the many beings.

And it is, of course, the heart of zazen, the heart of the Koan, the heart of shikantaza and of course the heart of our daily life, the Genjo Koan itself.

That kind of undivided activity is body-and-mind-heart engaged and involved as one **in the act**, the self completely forgotten, all the hands and eyes forgotten, the pillow itself forgotten.
Just that simple, natural act of reaching.

But for this to happen there must be one-ness, **intimacy with the basic need of reaching** for the pillow.

That basic and vital need, beyond any self-consciousness, beyond any idea, beyond any concept, any goal. that basic need of life and the many beings expressing freely itself.

Here we touch the heart of Kanzeon, the bodhisattva of compassion.
And compassion has the energy of practice and the energy of realisation itself.
Compassion is quite a stinky word, these daysCalmost lost its meaning.
I truly prefer "Love".

And it is interesting to go to the etymology of the word: com-passion.
It's not just the emotional feeling toward others, but "**com**", the prefix "com" is

"sharing", means "together".
And **passion** has two meanings: "suffering" and, of course, "passion" as passion.

So here the basic need of Kanzeon bodhisattva as our own intimate life and zazen is the perfectly natural act, n accord with the basic need of freedom for the many beings and ourselves as them, as an act of com-passion: together, sharing completely the suffering and the passion of life herself.

The primal passion of everyday life at the heart of zazen.

Dogen continues, saying, *About just such a moment you may suppose that because realisation is manifested in undivided activity, there was no realisation before this. However, before this realisation, undivided activity was manifested. Before this realisation, undivided activity was manifested*: throughout all space, throughout all time, all beings coming forth as undivided activity itself.

Throughout all space, throughout all time, zazen, shikantaza, the Koan, our very life coming forth as undivided activity itself.
This dialogue that we are quoting from the *Hekigan-Roku* continues with the teacher Dogo asking, in turn, to Ungan, *"How do you understand it?"*
How do you understand this action of Kanzeon bodhisattva?
Ungan said, *"The whole body is hand and eye"*.

This is a deeper point from the one that was before.

Before, it was said it is like a person in the middle of the night reaching for a pillow. Here, Ungan goes one step further: "The whole body is hand and eye" The whole body, the body of actuality; and this body of true nature as it is, intimate with the vastness, fullness, uniqueness and variety that is realisation before realisation, zazen before zazen, shikantaza before shikantaza, life before life.

That "before" is **oneness with the source**, moment by moment, forget-ting the self in the source, **as the source** itself...
Where the water is running fresh and clear.
"The whole body is hand and eye", says Master Ungan there. The whole body,

the whole zazen, is the perfectly natural basic need, passionate Love and compassion, that is joy itself manifesting fully in the act of hiding, in the intimate voice of the most intimate dharma companion that some may call Amitabha, limitless life, expressed fully and uniquely in the simple act of reaching for the pillow, breathing the Koan, blooming attention as shikantaza and every simple act in our simple daily life.

Dogen continues, saying, *But undivided activity manifested previously does not hinder the present realisation of undivided activity.*
Undivided activity manifested previously does not hinder the present realisation of undivided activity: not two, not different, not the same, we said yesterday.

Zazen, Koan, shikantaza, an act in our daily life as the act and quality of not hindering, not hindering birth, not hindering death, not hindering zazen from hiding in its own figure, which is this living moment's figure and form.
Undivided activity manifested previously does not hinder the present realisation of that wonderful undivided activity.

Dogen says in the *Genjo Koan*, "*To study the Buddha-Tao is to forget the self; to forget the self is to be actualised by the many beings. Body-and-mind as well as body-and-mind of others drop away. No trace of realisation remains, and this no-trace continues endlessly.*"
This no-trace continues endlessly, as the most deep and subtle stage of our zazen and life.
Indeed!!!

So here practice is to sit the body, sit the breathing, sit the mind-heart.

And the mind, that is the mountains and clouds and the rain and the wind, as that "**not-hindering**" itself, as that "**no-trace**" continuing endlessly.

That "no-trace" itself as the coming forth of the one that truly does zazen, the coming forth of the Tathagata, the most intimate companion.
There, *not one, not different* of this body and heart.
Dogen continues, saying, *Because of this your understanding can be manifested moment by moment.*

Because of that not-hindering, that no-trace of the person's realisation of undivided activity, because of this your understanding can be manifested or expressed, moment after moment in the real ground of practice and expression, our ordinary life, the Genjo Koan.

Here the dialogue from the *Hekigan-Roku* continues.
After the other teacher said, *"The whole body is hand and eye"*, Ungan said to him, *"How do you say it?"*
Dogo replied, taking one more step, *"Throughout the body, the hand and the eye"*.

Cheers!!!

So really, no need for us in this Sesshin, no need for us in zazen.
Sesshin does Sesshin, zazen does zazen, the Koan practises the Koan, shikantaza gives birth to itself.
"**Throughout the body, the hand and the eye**", the great bodhisattva, "Enlighten-ing Being", is moment by moment actualising traceless life.

Yes, as our very life.
This is our true home.
This is our true body and heart.
This is our true companion.

Our Latino Land story today says:
"There was once a man who would go every day to a bar and ask for two glasses of wine. Then he would sit and have a sip of one and then a sip of the other glass, and a sip of this, and a sip of the other one.
It continued for months.
And one day, he told the bartender why (who didn't dare to ask).
He said, "The most friend of my friends has gone away, so at the same hour he sits in his own place, I sit here, and we drink together".
So next day the same thing happened, and it continued for many, many days.
One day the man came and asked for just a glass of wine, and he sat there and sipped this only glass.
The bartender was quite moved, so he reached to the man and said, "I'm sorry

for your friend".

The man said, "Oh, no, no! He is well and alive, I am happy about that. It's only that I stopped drinking!"

So really, shedding off body-and-mind, forget-ting the self in the act, completely available for the ten thousand beings to advance and confirm the self, **we are not there**. We are not here, but someone, something, the great "Enlighten-ing Being" sits, walks, breathes, having that essential wine in intimate companionship with life, as *not one, not different*, not the same, not many.

Is there any other way of doing zazen?
Any other way of walking in life?
Is there really any other way for the freedom of the many beings?
For actualizing that essential freedom in and as our very life?

Let's appreciate that glass of wine...
Cheers!!!

Not to attain, not to know

Augusto Al Q'adi Alcalde
Sesshin, Teisho, Day 3

Dōgen Zenji, Shōbōgenzō: "Going beyond Buddha"

"Zen master Dao Wu visited the assembly of master Shitou.
Dao Wu asked, "What is the fundamental meaning of Buddha-dharma?"
Shitou said, "Not to attain, not to know".
Dao Wu said, "Is there some turning point in going beyond, or not?"
Shitou said, "The vast sky does not hinder the white clouds from flying"...
Shitou said, "Not to attain, not to know".
Understand that in Buddha-dharma the fundamental meaning
is in the first thought, as well as in the ultimate level.
This fundamental meaning is not-attaining.
It is not that there is no aspiration for enlightenment,
no practice, or no enlightenment.
But simply, there is not-attaining.
The fundamental meaning is not-knowing.
Practice–enlightenment is not nonexistent or existent,
but is not-knowing, not-attaining.
Again we say, the fundamental meaning is not attaining, not knowing.
It is not that there is no sacred truth, no practice–enlightenment,
but simply not-attaining, not-knowing...
"The vast sky does not hinder the white clouds from flying."
These are Shitou's words. The vast sky does not hinder the vast sky.
Just as the vast sky does not hinder the vast sky from flying, white clouds do not
hinder white clouds. White clouds fly with no hindrance.

White clouds' flying does not hinder the vast sky's flying.
Not hindering others is not hindering self...
Right now, raise the eyebrow of the eye of practice and study
and see through the coming forth of Buddhas, ancestors, self and others.
This is a case of asking one question and answering ten.
In asking one question and answering ten,
the person who asks one question is the true person;
the person who answers ten is the true person."

This is the chapter of "Going beyond Buddha", which is a text in the *Shōbōgenzō* by Dōgen Zenji. Basically, "Shōbōgenzō" means "eye and treasury of the true dharma" I see this chapter as very much appropriate for our third full day of sesshin, usually the turning point, the turning day in a long Sesshin.

But over the years I have noticed something very peculiar about these stages in a Sesshin, where we say the first day is like this, second day is like this, third day is like this, and so on.

What I have seen is that if the Sesshin is, say for example, a three-day Sesshin, the second day will be the turning point. And if it is a one-day Sesshin, in the middle of the day there will be some turning point.

So if this is so, and that turning point and the symptoms of the first day and the second day are really not fixed points, we can understand that **turning point is everywhere**; and also the symptoms of the first or the second day, or the seventh day are everywhere in our Sesshin.

We just say the third day is the turning point; but every moment, every breathing, every zazen is a turning point.
So here we are, the third day, third full day, facing the *Shōbōgenzō*.

Now we find Zen master Dao Wu here, visiting the assembly of master Shitou.
Dao Wu asked, "What is the fundamental meaning of Buddha-dharma?"
*Shitou said, "**Not to attain, not to know**".*

That's very interesting. In our four vows, we used to say "Buddha's way is beyond attainment; I vow to embody it fully".
And I think it has meaning, that thing about Buddha's way being beyond attainment.

It is just exactly the same point that is being said here, in the words of master Shitou: not-attaining, not-knowing—the fundamental meaning of the Buddha-dharma.

So if there is not-attaining and not-knowing as the fundamental meaning, what is that?
It is pointing to the **continuous returning** to what we can call **basic, primal sanity**—a kind of ground sanity, earth sanity, the sanity of primal roots: not attaining, not realising, and not understanding.

We call "It" Rebel Health, Sanity.

But also we have to be very careful not to interpret that as something lacking.

This "not to attain, not to know" is the mind of Bodhidharma facing the Emperor Wu, saying "I don't know" in front of The Question.
There we have Bodhidharma, 120 years old, coming from far away, facing the Emperor, and he just can say: "I don't know".

This is, of course, not merely ignorance, or not knowing how to answer; but **to be in intimate contact with the mystery itself**, and showing it without any kind of pollution: just "don't know".
I call that "basic sanity", and "rebel health" too.

We approach that basic sanity when we free ourselves from concepts of goals or progression along the path, even though they will naturally happen.

As Dōgen Zenji says, "You may practise Zen (Ch'an) forward, but you have to know that **each step is equal in substance**".

The tricky thing is that sometimes we reverse the meaning of that phrase, and so we dedicate our whole effort to practising forward, thinking that, in some moment, "each step that is equal in substance" will appear.
But the thing is already the reverse of that.

We practise "each step equal in substance", and suddenly, with surprise and joy, we find ourselves going forward.

So practice is the path itself, rather than the attainment of a so-called goal.

There we meet Shitou's mind: not to attain, not to know; returning once again to the "don't know" mind-heart, in which every single Koan is understood, seen and presented with the eyes and dance of primal innocence.

Primal Innocence: the intimate treasure of the Tao.

So here the path is the Tao, is what moment by moment inspires our lives, rather than the goal itself. We call it the Genjo Koan, the Koan of our everyday life.

The path, the Koan, shikantaza are not ahead, it, "she" is here; but right here, right now, breathing through our very body. Palpitating as our very heart.
You see: if not like this, if not now, when and where, then?

So thus in the Buddha Tao, "the Tao of Awakening", in the Buddha Way or "the "Awaken-ing Way" there is no goal at all; just that shedding off body and mind. And this happens when the 10,000 beings advance to the very bottom of oneself, to the very bottom of the universe. And touch it...

And then that "self", to call it in such a way, that innermost of the universe as our self, comes forward and liberates, frees, heals the many beings.

 Our text continues, saying: *Dao Wu said, "Is there some turning point in going beyond, or not?" Shitou said, "The vast sky does not hinder the white clouds from flying".*
And a bit further in the text, the same theme is taken again: *"The vast sky does not hinder the white clouds from flying".*
These are Shitou's words. The vast sky does not hinder the vast sky.

Just as the vast sky does not hinder the vast sky from flying, white clouds do not hinder white clouds.
White clouds fly with no hindrance.

Cheers!! lets dance.

Don't try to control them

Augusto Al Q'adi Alcalde
Sesshin, Teisho, Day 2

Only Buddha and Buddha
From the *Shobogenzo*, Chapter 5

> *"Long ago, a monk asked an old master:*
> *"When hundreds, thousands of myriads of objects come all at once,*
> *what should be done?"*
> *The master replied: "Don't try to control them".*
> *What he means is that in whatever way objects come,*
> *do not try to change them.*
> *Whatever comes is the Buddha dharma, not objects at all.*
> *Do not understand the master's reply as merely a brilliant admonition,*
> *but realise that it is the truth.*
> *Even if you try to control what comes, it cannot be controlled."*

Sit comfortably, if you need it.
OK. Here in our Sesshin, we meet Dogen again.

The name of the book we are working on today can be translated "Only Buddha and Buddha" or "Just Buddha and Buddha". I find it very interesting, especially for this day of Sesshin.

Normally the first day we establish ourselves, take root so to speak, make contact with the ground of Sesshin. So it is, I think, most appropriate for this day, this saying about controlling or changing what comes forth!

Here it says: *"Long ago, a monk asked an old master: "When hundreds, thousands of objects come all at once, what should be done?"*
This is not a special occasion. Maybe it is a special awareness of an everyday fact: hundreds, thousands of objects and beings coming all at once **just like now**.
And this refers to another phrase by Dogen Zenji, a very popular one, when he says: *"The ten thousand beings advancing and confirming, authenticating, the self"*. That, he says, we call realisation.
And he compares that **advancing** and **confirming**, "**actualizing-expressing**" the self by the ten thousand beings with another kind of living experience: *"That the self advances and confirms the many beings is called delusion.'*

As a matter of fact, he uses the expression "called" in the two of them: "*is called realisation*", "*is called delusion*". So we "*call it*" like that; but those two functions of our consciousness are quite natural.

We need the self advancing and confirming the many beings to live our everyday life. I need to call this a stick and this a Zafu and this, a Sesshin.
This is the self advancing and naming, confirming, the many beings. But for that to have a deep meaning in our life and practice, but we should realise the other side: that is, the ten thousand beings advance and confirm, authenticate, express, the self.

That living fact is present and shines when there is complete attention, complete openness, so that the actuality of this moment, the many beings that are also thoughts, feelings, sounds, dreams, , are coming forth and actualizing-expressing our own self.

Probably the monk was there in his own practice. He's gone past the fact of "the self advances and confirms the many beings" and he was, in his own zazen and life, in his own intimate Genjo Koan, in the other place: everything was advancing and going deep into himself, beyond himself.
So he goes to his teacher and says: *"When hundreds and thousands of objects and beings come all at once, what should be done?"*
The teacher said: *'Don't try to control them".*

Don't try to control them, that is also **don't attach to them,** don't even name them.

Don't try to direct them in any way!!!

It is at that point that Dogen says elsewhere: *"In attachment, blossoms fall. In aversion, weeds spread."*

So that *don't try to control them* also points to going beyond attachment or aversion.

We find at that point one thing that I am always saying: attention itself, which is zazen itself, cannot be maintained!!!

And the same is true for openness, because **the best thing we can do is to awaken it, to allow it to bloom, to burn completely into it.**

Attention, zazen, the Genjo Koan, our life, are then passion and Love with no centre or reference point, without territory map, the horizon herself walking as every step. There is hope here...

The uncertain certainty of True Nature, walking and inquiring as the "mist-ery" itself.

But once we try to direct or maintain it, it is already gone.

There is a case in the *Mumonkan* in which Nansen is asked about the Tao, and he says: *"If you try to direct to it, you deviate"*.

In other words, if you try to aim for it, you miss.

The Case continues, saying: *"What he means is that in whatever way objects come, do not try to change them."*

Here Dogen adds a new meaning to the phrase of the teacher. It is not only *"Don't try to control them"* but *"Do not try to change them"*.

And naming most of the times is really changing, given that "what comes forth" has no name.

It's just something that comes forth from emptiness itself, no name at all.

And we call, name it: we call it zazen, we call it bright zazen, we call it dull zazen, we call it first day, second day. And in this very calling, naming it, we change it, and the natural innocence of the living fact is lost.

"Don't try to change it." That points to the practice of seeing and living each thing, each moment, each encounter, just as it is.

That is the Tathagata coming forth, sweeping away all delusions, all doubts and all certainties.
And that happens if and when our body, mind and heart are ready.

What is that readiness we are talking about?

Readiness abides and expresses herself when no heart, no mind, no body are there to be found, just full attention opening.

There we find another phrase by Dogen Zenji that can be inspiring in our practice. He says: *"The entire universe is the dharma body of the self"*.
The "self" is the entire universe.

Not to change, not to control, the source of true transformative actions and steps, true revolutionary Zen.

And not only attention and openness, but we need for that also **respect and appreciation** for the unique quality of each being, each moment and each encounter.

This **body of uniqueness** is referred to as one of the three bodies of the Buddha, the Nirmanakaya, unique-varied-diverse...

So let us **wake up that respect and appreciation** to whatever is coming, without naming it as good or bad, bright or dull.

Of course, this leads naturally to what we call the third body of the Buddha, the Sambhogakaya, which is the full, joyful, passionate and complete quality of each being, each moment and each encounter.
So it is not only that it is unique, but also full and complete, full of joy and Love, this is to say alive.

"Not to control, not to change", Dogen is saying here.

That is, please do allow the actuality of the present moment to come forth as our own life, as our own body, our own mind, out true and intimate Genjo Koan.

There zazen meets this patchy quality of life, which is of course, as our zazen itself, unpredictable, uncertain and constantly alive.

So what is the way in which we can sit and live in that not-controlling, not-changing practice? The only way is not to be there!!!

The same way that the best way of doing zazen is not being there, really not doing zazen: body-heart and mind shedding off, away, and just zazen, just life, just the Genjo Koan is happening, not "we" ourselves "doing it" or "going through" this Sesshin.

Zazen does and express the Sesshin; the Koan does and express the Sesshin; shikantaza does and express the Sesshin.
We have no part there.
In that way, body and heart-mind disappear in each spark of attention, each moment of endless practice and life.

"Whatever comes is the Buddha dharma, not objects at all"
Whatever comes is the Buddha dharma, not objects at all!!!

We had that expression: "Tathagata", which is one way the Buddha used to refer to himself, and literally meaning **"that which thus comes"**.
That is the point when Dogen says: *"Whatever comes is the Buddha dharma"*, the Tathagata.
And in seeing that we met the place in which we can really wake up this sense of appreciation and containment that we are talking about.

"Do not understand the master's reply as merely a brilliant admonition, but realise that it is the truth", says Dogen Zenji.

"Even if you try to control what comes, it cannot be controlled." That's a very interesting phrase.

Even if you try to control and change what comes, it cannot be controlled, just cannot be controlled.
It looks here as if Dogen Zenji was speaking about my old bike!
But it is not just that.
It's the true nature of reality.
And that is our hope, that is our opening.

If essential nature were just a matter of riding it, it would be our own creation, which as Harada Daiun Roshi said "has not power to save horses or donkeys".

So zazen is not conflict, nor is it a struggle between what is now and our idea of what should be.
Sitting with no control in heart body and mind, there is only attention, and our skin does not separate our-selves from the vast universe and the vast dharma itself: only zazen, only the Genjo Koan, only shikantaza, with the observer, the actor, shedding off in the act and expression of understanding its own insubstantiality.

There is pregnancy here.

At that point of **wonder and aliveness**, there is never an entire universe that is not our-selves, but the dharma body, the body of the Tao itself.

The monk says: "*When hundreds, thousands of objects and beings come all at once, what should be done?*"
What should be done?

There is a poem that says:
Full moon;
everything wet with dew
except the dew itself.

Let us be true to this.
Cheers!!!

If it is not

   the practice with all beings...

"Only Buddha and Buddha"

Augusto Al Q'adi Alcalde
Zen Intensive, Talk 2

Good.. here we are in our third full day in this Intensive and my intention was to continue with the *"identity of time and being"* essay by Dogen but distraction took me to another chapter.

So today I want to take up some words by Dogen Zenji from an essay that follows this "identity of time being", and it's called *"**Only Buddha and Buddha.**"* And the first quotation from there says like this:

"A Buddha's practice is to practice in the same manner as the entire universe and all beings. If it is not the practice with all beings it is not the Buddha's practice."

It is very very interesting, and gives us the possibility of deepening what we have been enquiring these previous days.

 "A Buddha's practice is to practice in the same manner as the entire universe and all beings. If it is not the practice with all beings it is not the Buddha's practice," he says very clearly.
So what is this practice?.

It is just and only the practice **with**, or "the practice **of the with**" itself as zazen, as life, as our very Genjo Koan.

The practice **with** all beings, not away, or apart, or against, or beyond something, but *with* all beings.

If it is not the practice with all beings it is not Buddha's practice, says Dogen here.

And Buddha also means Awaken-ing, so it is not awakened or awakening practice if it does not happen like that, if it is not engaged like this, embodied like this, expressed like this.

So **what is the quality** of that "**with**" that he is pointing to here? What is it?

That "quality" is our very life, our very body and heart, the true companion of each true step and dance.

Another quotation says *"The mountains, rivers and earth are born at the same moment with each person. All Buddha's of the past future and present are practicing together with each person."*

Another interesting paragraph.

"The mountains, rivers and earth are born at the same moment with each person, this is, each one of us.

"All Buddhas of the past future and present are practicing together **with** each person." Each one of us!.

So we asked what is the quality of this '**With**"?

It is the quality of **intimacy**.

Each **one** of us...

Just one body; just one heart, just one life, no self, no other.

A vast fearless inclusive open identity as our Zazen, our Shikantaza or our Koan practice.

A vast fearless inclusive open identity as our very life and living.

Dogen says elsewhere that all beings of all directions, the ten directions, do come forth and **actualize the self as practice**.

Actualize True Nature as practice.

Just the many beings, from all directions and all times, wonderfully coming forth and actualizing the self; making the self actual, real, now.
Our life being the expression and realization of the actual; the real, the now...

And he also has something to say about this Self thing in this essay: *"What Buddha has called the Self is the entire universe. There is never an entire universe that is not the self with or without our knowing it. It doesn't depend on knowing."*

What Buddha has called **the Self is the entire universe** so this is what is actualised in our life, our Genjo Koan, our Zazen.

When all beings do come forth and actualize the Self, the entire universe is actualized at and as the very single, simple and wholehearted **act**.

"There is never an entire universe that is not the Self with or without our knowing. The mountains, the rivers and the earth are born at the same moment and do come to life at the same moment with each person. All Buddha's of the past future and present are practicing together with each person".

Thus the **person** is born in that **act** that we call Zazen.

The new world, the new universe is born here.
The heart is born, the body is born
So we touch and express Shikantaza as life and walking.

Motionless; complete body-heart-mind, abiding in and as **open inclusive attention;** as **fearlessness** and **loving intimacy with this moment**.

This is the **Why** we are here, this is the **What** we are here; this is **How** we are here.
Our common and intimate purposeless meaningful sharing.

The mountains rivers and earth are born at the same moment with each person and everything is practicing together which each one of us but greed, rejection ignorance tries to abide in "permanence" and "security" by separation.
An illusory intention or movement: not to acknowledge-wake up to, embody

and be embodied by this creative birthing of the mountains, rivers, earths, person, in a moment to moment Awaken-ing.

Then fear and self centeredness tries to avoid this realization, which is the realization of **Us**, as community itself.
This fear tries to avoid community by burning bridges.
But if we try to avoid community by burning bridges then fire is our community.

And certainly it is **loving intimacy** with this moment that we are talking about when we talk about the **Why**, the **What**, the **How** we are here, our common and intimate purposeless meaningful sharing.

Cheers to that!!!

It would not be trustworthy

Augusto Al Q'adi Alcalde
Sesshin, Day 3

"Only Buddha and Buddha"
By Dogen Zenji

"Buddha dharma cannot be known by a person.
For this reason, since olden times no ordinary person
has realised Buddha Dharma.
No practitioner of the lesser vehicles has mastered Buddha Dharma.
Because it is realised by Buddhas alone, it is said only a Buddha and a Buddha
can completely master it.
When you realise Buddha Dharma, you do not think:
This is a realisation just as I expected.
Even if you think so, realisation always differs from your expectation.
Realisation is not like your conception of it.
Accordingly, realisation cannot take place as previously conceived.

When you realise Buddha Dharma,
you do not consider how realisation came about.
You should reflect on this. What you think, one way or another,
before realisation is not a help for realisation.
Although realisation is not like any of the thoughts preceding it,
this is not because such thoughts were actually bad and could not be realisation.
Past thoughts in themselves were already realisation.
But since you were seeking elsewhere, you thought and said that thoughts
cannot be realisation. However, it is worth noticing that

what you think one way or another is not a help for realisation.
Then you are careful not to be small-minded. If realisation came forth
by the power of your prior thoughts, it would not be trustworthy.
Realisation does not depend on thoughts, but comes forth far beyond them.
Realisation is helped only by the power of realisation itself.
Know that then there is no delusion and there is no realisation."

Please sit comfortably, if you need it.
OK. We continue our disorderly hopping through the *Shobogenzo*.

Yesterday I think we had Chapter 5 and now we have Chapter 1. Anyway, the same book, "Only Buddha and Buddha".

Dogen Zenji begins by saying: *"Buddha dharma cannot be known by a person. For this reason, since olden times no ordinary person has realised Buddha Dharma".*
Believe it or not, this is not a discouraging affirmation. *Buddha Dharma cannot be known by a person* is perfectly pointing to true practice.

"Cannot be known", he is saying here, and this is the key and the path, as well as the walking.

And it reminds me of a saying by Master Shitou, who said: *"The fundamental meaning of Buddha Dharma is not to attain, not to know".*
That is really pointing to the **unknown**, the **mystery**, but not the unknown that **can** be known; not that mystery that **can** be solved, but the one that cannot be known, just because that's its true nature: **"cannot be known"**.

This is the potency, the embodying and the expression of True Nature.

There we walk the Question, and the Question is walking us, and each common step and heartbeat is allowing the Pure Land, the "Land with No Evil" of our Ancestors in this Land, to bloom and fill all space and time.
Our True Body, **as** all beings and Mother Earth.

Always fresh; always new; never an object of knowledge, something to deposit into our brain.

"The Buddha Dharma cannot be known", says Dogen Zenji here.
And this is not far away: that *"cannot be known"* is just "leaves are green, flowers are red", expressing clearly, intimately the mystery and joy as well as the walking of the pregnant unknown.

So what is the mystery of life and the mystery of our own practice?
"Cannot be known by a person". We can see two kinds of meaning in that word **"person"**, the same as we can see two persons; which is not to say that they are different, but two sides of the same reality in each one of us.

One of them, one of those persons, is the one that is made up by the five skandhas, as we say when we recite every day in our *Hannya Shin Gyo, the Heart Sutra*.

That makes up in time as we grow and become adults: our conditioned mind, with its natural anxiety, fear, expectation, resentments, wishes and dislikes, always searching for continuity, something secure to hold on to, some affirmation.

That is one kind of **"person"**, always reacting from the mechanical mind, from the ashes of the past, never thus being responsible and responsive to the now, responsible and responsive to the actuality of this very moment.

And, as Aitken Roshi points out elsewhere, responsibility is ability to respond. We cannot respond if we are clouded by our memories, expectations, wishes or concepts. And i know well about this!!!

The other is Rinzai Zenji's **"True Person with No-Rank"**
"True person with no marks or characteristics at all".
He says: *"In that lump of flesh and bones, there is a true person always going in and out through our senses"*.

That person is the one in which our practice can take shelter for understanding the Buddha Dharma.
That is the point of what Dogen Zenji says: *"Because it is realised by Buddhas alone, it is said only a Buddha and a Buddha can completely master it"*.
It is realised by Buddhas alone: there the true person realises the true person,

Buddhas realise Buddhas, and the Buddha Dharma realises the Buddha Dharma itself.

And it is not being said here that we get *transformed* into Buddhas, that we "ordinary beings" get transformed into Buddhas at that moment.

Only that we take shelter in it, become one with our true reality, the true fact, the true joy that Hakuin Zenji is pointing at when he says: "**This very body is the Buddha**".

There the Buddha Dharma is not only realised, but also personalised, which I think is the most important part of our practice as expression and walking. Personalise it as our-selves, as the entire universe as the infinity of the walking, the immensity and inclusivity of the horizon.

Just as infinite, immense and inclusive as this very heartbeat, this leaf, this dog bark, this very moment.

"When you realise the Buddha Dharma, do not think: `This is realisation, just as I expected`. Even if you think so, realisation always differs from your expectation. Realisation is not like your conception of it. Accordingly, realisation cannot take place as previously conceived".
"This is realisation, just as I expected", do not think like that, says Dogen Zenji.

Expectations and conceptions come from the past, which is the known, which is just memory. And to quote Bankei Zenji, the unborn that he was always talking about through all this teachings and life, the unborn that constantly is coming into life as our very life, our practice, which is completely fresh, and free.

It's not subject to expectations or concepts.
It is the fire and the flames, not the ashes.

And, you know, after all, what can be more disappointing than to realise that realisation is just as we expected! Boring, indeed!

"Cannot take place as previously conceived". Really, **cannot** take place.
This is a strong affirmation; like the one that says: *"What you think is not a help for realisation"*. Really, if there is a clear previous concept about how things

should be, how realisation should manifest itself, these concepts are occupying a place in which realisation can sit and do Mu and do shikantaza instead, do our zazen as everyday life.

He says: *"What you think is not a help for realisation"*, but we should understand also that it is not an obstruction.
This "just thinking" doesn't help, doesn't block.

How can it block the power and pregnancy of the unknown?

"Although realisation is not like any of the thoughts preceding it, this is not because such thoughts were actually bad and could not be realisation. Past thoughts in themselves were already realisation."
Past thoughts in themselves were already realisation itself, he is saying.

He is here pointing to **the thought itself**, and not to the chain of "thinking about"; just the thought, **just that flashing moment of the mind in the now**.

This is what we call also **"Nen"**: every day we chant the *Enmei Jikku Kannon Gyo*, expressing "Nen nen fu ri shin": *"the mind in the now (nen), the thought in the now (nen), is one with the heart-mind, comes from the mind-heart"*.

At that point we can just see a thought as realisation itself, a flash of mind in a moment as realisation itself. There we find and express our True Body and Heart.

"Since you were seeking elsewhere, you thought and said that thoughts cannot be realisation". We were searching around, and in that way we couldn't recognise what was already manifesting itself, brand new vividly clear.

Since you were seeking elsewhere, you thought and said that thoughts cannot be realisation; that your actual mind cannot be realisation. This is projecting our Genjo Koan or our shikantaza or our zazen, our life, into the future, practising as if the Buddha Dharma, the Buddha Tao-Way were a kind of Star Trek.
And it is not like that.

In that way we don't pay attention to Ikkyu's advice, very simple, very effective: **"Attention, attention, attention"**.

There is a story, in the Muslim Sufi tradition, in which a person was searching for something in the garden, and a friend comes and says to him: "What are you searching for?" He said: "I am searching for the key of my house, the door of my house". So the guy decides to help the other.
And several hours after, he asks: "So, where did you lose the key?"
And the other guy says: "Oh, I lost the key in that other place".
So the friend is really upset and says: "So why are we searching here?"
And the other says: "Because in that place it's dark, and this place has more light".

This is a basic temptation and attitude in our practice: to settle down in those so-called "bright" places.
But this is not the place where we lost the thing.

We should go to the dark places, that dark cave, the "mouth of the wolf" that Hakuin says is the mirror of wisdom.
Really there is nothing terrible about that dark mouth of the wolf.

Nothing is darker than the obvious, nothing more obvious than the actuality of the present moment as life, as practice, as us.

"However, it is worth noticing that what you think one way or another is not a help for realisation. Then you are careful not to be small-minded. If realisation came forth by the power of your prior thoughts, it would not be trustworthy."
That's a very interesting phrase: *"If realisation came forth by the power of your prior thoughts, it would not be trustworthy"*.
It would be just our own creation.

Elsewhere, in the *Mumonkan*, there is a phrase that says: *"Things that are the result of cause and effect go away because of cause and effect"*.

Every single thing that we **produce** through our practice, which we create through our practice, will go away. That's for sure.

So the Buddha Dharma is not concerned with that kind of realisation that can be just the projection of our ideas or concepts about that. At all.

There is a story about a chicken that after hard practice was able to become a fox.
That was just what she wanted.
And at that moment, she discovered, with utter disappointment, that she was not able any more to eat corn!

Sometimes this is the nature of transformation: we become a fox, but we still want to eat corn.
Corn is our true nature...

This happens when we are just creating a ground first and then we walk through it and then we reach some place.
That is possible.
It happens every moment.
But that is not the true thing.

 "Realisation does not depend on thoughts, but comes forth far beyond them".
"Realisation is helped only by the power of realisation itself." "Does not depend on thoughts, but comes forth far beyond them".

From the limits of the limitless universe, the Koan comes forth, shikantaza comes forth; from the most intimate of our self, the Genjo Koan comes forth, shikantaza comes forth, filling all life, all time, all space as our common True Body-Heart.
Realisation there *"is helped only by the power of realisation itself"*, says Dōgen Zenji.
What is that power of realisation itself?

Rinzai Zenji has something to say there: *"When I am hungry, I eat; when I am tired, I sleep"*.
This is true power. This is true realisation.

No technique or method can produce total attention, genuine realisation.
This is not a promised result, just as love is not.

Just to see intimately, with our whole body-and-mind, the complete dance of non-attention clouding the aliveness and completeness of each moment, is attention itself, is practice itself, is realisation itself.

Our text finishes, saying: *"Know that then there is no delusion and there is no realisation"*.
We say here there is no realisation.
And I say at this very moment there is no delusion.

There comes to my mind a poem that says:

> *For those who wait only for flowers to bloom,*
> *I wish I could show them the spring grass*
> *under the snow of a mountain village.*

The spring grass under the snow of a mountain village: let us settle there.
Come and dance!!!

Cheers!!!

In the same manner as the entire universe and all beings

Augusto Al' Qadi Alcalde
Sesshin, Day 6

Dogen Zenji, "Only Buddha and Buddha"

"This is how to understand.
Is there anyone who knows what birth in its beginning or end is like?
No-one knows either birth's end or its beginning. Nevertheless, everyone is born.
Similarly, no-one knows the extremities of mountains, rivers and earth;
but all see this place and walk here.
Do not think with regret that the mountains, rivers and earth are not born with
you. Understand that the ancient Buddha teaches that your birth is
non-separate from the mountains, rivers and earth.
Again, all Buddhas of the three worlds have already practised,
attained the way and completed realisation.
How should we understand that those Buddhas are practising together with us?

First of all, examine a Buddha's practice.
A Buddha's practice is to practise in the same manner as the entire universe
and all beings. If it is not practice with all beings, it is not a Buddha's practice.
This being so, all Buddhas, from the moment of attaining realisation, realise
and practise the way together with the entire universe and all beings.
You may have doubts about this, but the ancient Buddha's word
was expounded in order to clarify your confused thinking.
Do not think that Buddhas are other than you."

Please sit comfortably, if you need.

So here today we focus once again on a part of the *Shobogenzo*'s essay called "Only Buddha and Buddha": *This is how to understand. Is there anyone who knows what birth in its beginning or end is like? No-one knows either birth's end or its beginning. Nevertheless, everyone is born.*

Here Dogen Zenji is focusing on the **"how"**.

Thus he begins saying: This is **how** to understand.
How to under-stand.

And the **how** is the **what**; the **how** is the **when**; the **how** is the **who** to understand.
It is understanding as expression and creativity herself.

And thus also the "how" is the "**relation-ship**", what we call **intimate Indra's Net**.

The "how to understand" is the relationship and the intimate quality of that relationship itself, the vital relationship between Buddha and the star; the vital relationship between Dogen and shedding off body and mind; the vital relationship between Joshu and the oak tree in the garden.

The ear and the bell sound, the ass and the Zafu, the Genjo Koan and everyday life. That is truly Indra's Net.

So let's forget completely about the jewel. There are lots of talk about jewels and diamonds!

But our practice happens in the Net itself, that powerful ground of the relationship in which the star can and can teach us, in which the dropped away body and mind can walk and dance on the earth.

In which the oak tree in the garden stands there without shadow, liberating the many beings, and establishing right here and now the Pure Land, the Land with No Evil of our ancestors that is so badly needed in this greedy and ignorant neo-liberal shitstem (quoting brother Peter Tosh's words) of this days.

So let us forget about the jewel, and lets bring forth, through our whole body-heart-mind and walking attention, our zazen, to life into and as everyday life, the very Genjo Koan itself, that very Net.

That very heart walking.
That Net that is essentially no gap.

And is the heart and walking of the Mist-ery, the Don't-know mind.

Dogen continues his rap saying, *no-one knows either birth's end or its beginning. Nevertheless, everyone is born. Similarly, no-one knows the extremities of the mountains, rivers and earth, but all see this place and walk here.*

No-one knows: that is the mind, heart and expression of the mystery.

No-one knows. vast and fathomless don't-know, the heart-mind and inquiring of primal innocence, the black female of the Tao Te Ching, the Mysterious Gate of all Wonders and Creations.

Here in zazen, in the Genjo Koan that is our very life (and please be clear I said "our"...) we realise the form, the intimate form of that heart-mind, the don't-know mind.

How ancient or newly born is that mind?
What is the face of the mystery?
How does it dance the Rumba?
How does it walks expressing the revolutions?

How much of that vast and fathomless innocence we cover with each step?

No-one knows the extremities of the mountains, rivers and earth, but all see this place and walk here, says Dogen.

But all see this place and walk here! This is about **expression**.

And they say, "to be mature in Zen is to be mature in expression".
This is expression itself, and expression is maturity, that maturity that is not born from age or time; that wholeness of mind, heart and body in which there is no place for options.

And just because of that, the mist-ery, the Buddha dharma, has a chance for establishing right here, right now, the Pure Land, liberating the many beings as ourselves from suffering, walking thus the Land with No Evil.

We all see this place and walk here, says Dogen.

All see this place and walk here, without knowing end or beginning or extremity for life, mountains, earth, oceans.

That is the shape of our common intimate Zen heart and walking.

In another text, the Shobogenzo says: *"No matter how far a fish swims, there is no end to the water. No matter how far a bird flies, there is no end to the space."*.
Seeing **this** place and walking **here**, we touch the **how** that we were focusing on here. The **"how"**.

There Dogen has also something to say: *"Know that water is life and space is life. Bird is life and fish is life."*
And he continues, saying: *"Do not think with regret that the mountains, rivers and earth are not born with you. Understand that the ancient Buddha teaches that your birth is non-separate from the mountains, rivers and earth"*.

Wonderful fact! Your birth is non-separate from the mountains, rivers and earth!!!
Birth is not separate from the mind, that heart that is the mountains, the oceans, the rivers and our own intimate mind-heart inquiring and walking.

And that mind-heart that is our body, actualising moment by moment the Genjo Koan, the "fundamental point".

Birth is not separate from the mind, says Dogen. Thus the "how" is **intimacy** with that mind.

The "what" is the mystery itself.

The "when", this very moment, newly born, freshly alive.

And the "who" is the "how", that very mind, mountains, rivers, earth and its many beings, sitting as the Koan, as shikantaza.

Walking and expressing the Land as the Genjo Koan, our very life.

Not "as if", but intimately **as** the mountains.

"As if" is the disgrace of Zen and life.

Dogen continues, saying: "*Again, all Buddhas of the three worlds have already practised, attained the way and completed realisation. How should we understand that those Buddhas are practising together with us? First of all, examine a Buddha's practice. A Buddha's practice is to practise in the same manner as the entire universe and all beings. If it is not practice with all beings, it is not a Buddha's practice*".
Very interesting.

A Buddha's practice is to practise in the same manner as the entire universe and all beings. If it is not practice with all beings, it is not a Buddha's practice. **In the same manner**, he says...

And elsewhere also, in the Genjo Koan, "Actualizing the fundamental point" the Shobogenzo says: "*If a bird or a fish tries to reach the end of its element before moving in it, this bird or fish will not find its way or its place. When you find your place right there where you are, practice happens, actualising the fundamental point. When you find your way at this moment, practice happens, actualising the fundamental point. Here is the place, here the way unfolds.*"

So clear that there is no need to spoil it with any comment. "Here is the place, here the way unfolds."

Thus the practice of the entire universe and all beings is life itself, limitless life, filling all space and time.

And that's the nature and body of our Zen, that's the nature of our Koan, that's the nature of our shikantaza, hte nature of our everyday life and walking.
Some call it Amitabha Buddha, limitless-life Buddha.
I tend to agree...

Dogen continues, saying: *"This being so, all Buddhas, from the moment of attaining realisation, realise and practise the way together with the entire universe and all beings"*.

At the moment of attaining realisation, the moment in which old Gautama sang *"**Wonderful living fact!** All beings throughout space and time have the wisdom and compassion of the Tathagata, and at this very moment have attained the way."* Wisdom and compassion of the Tathagata, of the "what thus comes, and thus goes".

Just like the sound of the rain, like the sun, like the clouds, like one single thought, like one single Koan.
This is the Tathagata coming and going, full of Love, full of wisdom.

So, *all Buddhas from the moment of attaining realisation realise and practise the way **together** with the entire universe and all beings.*

That is how the Buddha realised that all beings at this very moment have attained the way.
That truly indeed is **"together"**, togetherness beyond space and time.

Practising the way, the Tao; actualising Love and wisdom, expressing and walking them for a new world and horizon.

Again, with this **"together"** we touch and express the Net; "together" is "no-gap"; "together" is "nothing lacking".
No-thing lacking!!!

Together is just one Genjo Koan, just one living moment of shikantaza, engaging and involving fully body, heart and walking, so that "the white heron in the snowfield hides itself in its own form", and the whole universe comes forth as our zazen, our very everyday life.

The Shobogenzo continues, saying: *"You may have doubts about this, but the ancient Buddha's word was expounded in order to clarify your confused thinking. Do not think that Buddhas are other than you".*

Do not think that Buddhas are other than you!!!
No other than you.

You, which is a form of the "us", are not other than Buddhas inquiring beyond certainties and answers, walking, blooming the new Land.

But let us forget all this talk about you-others.
Let us forget about the Buddhas.
Let us forget, shed off the self, and **be actualised by that very act** of shedding off the self.

Only the Genjo Koan, only zazen, only shikantaza, only that bow, that step at kinhin.

Only this precious and unique living moment of our life, our Genjo Koan beating and breathing as our very heart and lungs. And Love.

Lets then appreciate our life, there is no Zen besides this.

Old man Antonio says:

"Do not get tired asking when your road and walking will end.
Right there when the yesterday and the morrow met and unite,
right there it will be completed"

Met you there!
Where? Here!!!

Cheers!

Chopping down is nothing other than chopping down

Augusto Al Q'adi Alcalde
Sesshin, Day 7

Dogen Zenji, "Only Buddha and Buddha"

"A teacher of old said, Chopping down is nothing other than chopping down.
Moving about is just that. Mountains, rivers and earth are
the entirely revealed body of the dharma king.
A person of the present should study this phrase of the teacher of old.
There is a dharma king who understands that the body of the dharma king
is not different from chopping down,
just as mountains are on earth and the earth is holding up mountains.
When you understand, a moment of no-understanding
does not come and hinder understanding,
and understanding does not break no-understanding.
Instead, understanding and no-understanding are just like spring and autumn.
However, when you do not understand,
the pervasive voice of the dharma does not reach your ears.
In the midst of the voice, your ears dally about.
But when you understand, the voice has already reached your ears,
Samadhi has emerged.
Know that no-understanding cannot be discerned by a self.
The dharma king's understanding is just like this.
In the dharma king's body, the eye is just like the body,
and the mind is the same as the body.

There is not the slightest gap between mind and body;
everything is fully revealed".

Please sit comfortably, if you need it.

A teacher of old said, Chopping down is nothing other than chopping down.
Moving about is just that. Mountains, rivers and earth are the entirely revealed
body of the dharma king.

That is the beginning of this chapter of "Only Buddha and Buddha".
Dogen is here quoting another teacher who says *Chopping down is nothing*
other than chopping down.

Nothing other. This is to express: "*Moving about is just that".*

And also is sitting, running, doing or doing nothing living and breathing, our
intimate Genjo Koan.

"Nothing other" and "just this" are basically the subtle meaning of **Shikan**,
"just", "nothing but", "**nothing extra**".

Chopping down is nothing other than chopping down, just that whole single
passionate and loving act, involving and engaging fully body heart and mind,
engaging and inviting the aliveness of this very moment, joining the Dance,
expressing as that single act of chopping down, as the single act of Gassho, the
single act of scratching our head.

That **single act of our whole body and heart** reveals, expresses the body of the
dharma king, says Dogen Zenji here.
And that dharma king or queen sits zazen and walks through life and the Genjo
Koan as the mountains, rivers, earth, completely revealed.
Nothing lacking.

"*A person of the present should study this phrase of the teacher of old",*
continues our text." *There is a dharma king who understands that the body of*
the dharma king is not different from chopping down, just as mountains are on
earth and the earth is holding up mountains". The body of the dharma king is

not different from chopping down, not different from the act itself.
Even more, we can say the act is what brings forth the body of the dharma king.

The body is the act.
The mind is the act, the heart is the act.
There we can say truly, "We, this food and our eating are empty".
The so-called "Three Wheels"; we, the food, our eating.

Just the act of chopping down; just the act of breathing the Koan.

Just the act of waking up a moment of shikantaza, just the act of walking our Genjo Koan.

The body of the dharma king is not different from chopping down. Neither is ours...

When you understand, a moment of no-understanding does not come and hinder understanding, says Dogen here.

"When you understand"...
Where is that **when**?

It is beyond time, and yet completely actual, completely alive, abiding into and as this fresh moment of Genjo Koan, this fresh moment of shikantaza.
This fresh and brand new moment of life and living.

Can we appreciate this? Can we express this?

Hope so, and not only for ourselves, but for the sake of the horizon, the kids, animals, plants, the Mother Earth and the necessary Dreams.

And at the same time, with deep and intimate roots into the timeless moment, beyond history, beyond even Shakyamuni Buddha himself, realising that all beings have the wisdom and compassion of the tathgata and have attained, at this very moment, the Way

With deep and intimate roots into the timeless Love and Heart, that timeless moment of the Seven Ancient Awakened Ones realize and express that all beings have the wisdom and compassion of the Tathagata and have attained, expressed, at this very moment, the Tao.

That is "**when**".
When we understand, *a moment of no-understanding does not come and hinder understanding.*
That phrase, "no-understanding", is a phrase that Dogen uses in other essays of the *Shobogenzo*, and has a special meaning.

"No-understanding", in Sino-Japanese, is "**fu e**", and the meaning of that is "**neither apart from, nor separated by, subject/object dichotomy or duality**".
Hence the meaning is "intimate understanding".

"No-understanding", "fu-e" as "Intimate understanding".
So he is saying that **a moment of completely intimate understanding does not come and hinder understanding**.

That is the alive meeting of the mysteries.

The meeting of understanding and intimate understanding itself, like two arrows meeting in the empty sky.
Just like this moment, right here and now.

Very interesting.

"*U*nderstanding *does not break no-understanding. Instead, understanding and intimate understanding are just like spring and autumn*", he says.
Just as spring and autumn.

And elsewhere we find, "*Do not suppose that what you realise becomes your knowledge and is grasped by your consciousness. Although actualised immediately, the inconceivable may not be apparent. Its appearance is beyond your knowledge*".

Truly, indeed.
Just as spring and autumn, just as the meeting of understanding and intimate understanding.

Spring is in a flower, autumn is in a falling leaf.
It doesn't matter when it really happens.

The ripeness of time brings forth the flower and the falling leaf, and we can realise that this happens truly beyond time.
And express this as our very body, our very heart, our very walking.

"Do not suppose that what you realise becomes your knowledge and it is grasped by your consciousness. Its appearance is beyond our knowledge, just like spring and autumn. However, continues our text, *when you do not understand, the pervasive voice of the dharma does not reach your ears. In the midst of the voice, your ears dally about. But when you understand, the voice has already reached your ears and Samadhi has emerged".*

Samadhi has emerged…

It says also, *"When you paint spring, do not paint willows, do not paint plums, peaches or apricots. Just paint spring. Do not use other means, but let plum blossoms initiate spring".*

If we are painting zazen and the Genjo Koan, do not paint Mu, do not paint breathing, do not paint "correct posture".

Just let plum blossoms initiate spring.
Just let intimacy initiate spring.

Just let this alive moment wake up our living and walking, our Genjo Koan, our shikantaza.
Samadhi has already emerged.

"Know that no-understanding (intimate understanding) *cannot be discerned by a self,* it says. *The dharma king's understanding is just like this".*
Intimate understanding cannot be discerned by a self.
True true true…

We meet in the *Genjo Koan* the following phrase: *"When you see forms or hear sounds, fully engaging body and mind, you understand them intimately".*

Fully engaging body, mind, heart, we understand intimately. Can't do it without Love, can't do it without passion...

Here we find body and mind shedding off into intimacy, into the alive mystery that is the dharma gate of ease and joy.

There is no self to find there.
Just intimacy, abiding nowhere, coming forth, not clearing up the mystery but making the mystery clear.
The Mist-ery walking us leaving no trace.
Just like ordinary life...

"In the dharma king's body, the eye is just like the body, and the mind is the same as the body. There is not the slightest gap between mind and body. Everything is fully revealed".

The eye is just like the body.
The mind and the heart is the same as the body.

"There is only a Buddha's single eye, which is itself the entire universe", says Dogen elsewhere.
That single eye, which is itself the entire universe, is just like the body. Just like our very life, expressing wholly the mist-ery, the traceless Tao of ease and joy.

There is hope there and there is a horizon there. Please dive!!!

Everything that comes forth from the study of the Way is the true human body, he says.
"True human body".

Everything that comes through study and practice of the Way, **that** is the body; and the heart and mind are the same as the body.

"There is not the slightest gap between mind and body. Everything is fully revealed", it says at the end our chapter here.

There is not the slightest gap between heart-mind and body.
That is the ground of the Koan, true intimate Genjo Koan, beyond practice and

"attainment".
That is shikantaza beyond shikantaza.

No-gap sitting, no-gap walking, no-gap breathing, as the Genjo Koan, as shikantaza and life itself.
There is not the slightest gap between mind, heart and body, so **everything is fully revealed**.

No gap.

A bird flies like a bird, a fish swims like a fish.

Each moment of zazen, each Koan, each shikantaza, each step in this walking that we call Zen is equally wholeness of practice-expression, wholeness of realisation.
There is no gap.

The old plum tree suddenly opens and the world of blossoming flowers arises.
Can we smell them?
Give you a clue: they can smell like sweat and laugh, and they love and walk.

The world of blossoming flowers arises, what do you see in the mirror?

Cheers!!!

The Virtue of the Tao's Herb

By Augusto Al Q'adi Alcalde

From the "Autumn Bridge Dojo"

I have been chewing one of Dogen's experiences and phrases through the Shobogenzo. And that phrase. **"Do Toku"**, was shining.

There are many possible translations of that Do Toku, but of course, enough to say, the only real "translation" is the living experience of it. The "common" living experience, the social one, the one that has the power to change our hearts and the world.

The usual one is **"Total Dedication"**, Total, full dedication.

But the words themselves, the ideographs themselves are quite interesting. **Do** is the same as Zen**do** or the **way** or the **Tao**. And **Toku** is the equivalent for **Teh** in **Tao Teh King**.

It is the power, or energy, or "virtue", of the Tao.

We could also translate not only as "total dedication" but also as **"total availability"**, to practice and essential nature. Our Zapatista brothers and sisters do say "the word is half of the one who says it, and half of the one who hears." Thus, our "hearing" reality and our common heart, does create reality, makes our true nature shine.

May I quote Jun Fan? (also known as Bruce Lee) "Wu Hsin, No Mind, consists in a subtle art of harmonizing the mind's essence with the essence of the place and situation in which we are working and doing. The innermost secret awaits for the silence"

So we can say that this is the **power** or **energy** or virtue, and not in the moral sense of the word "virtue" but as potential, as in what is the "virtue" of this plant or this herb.
The virtue of the Tao.

The Tao. We shouldn't forget, if we understand what Lao Tzu is saying in his little book, it is the unknown, is the nameless, is the black female, the mother of all mystery.

Dogen talks about this total dedication as one of the fundamental elements of Zazen, the formless actualization of Unconditional Attention. Or, as a friend said, "making Love to emptiness" right on!!!

Completely disappearing **into** Zazen, into and as that very Attention as our True Body and Heart, this living moment.
Completely disappearing **into** each breath, **each** moment, **each** step.

As them.

Total dedication.

I think this is related with the word "Intensive" or intense that we use to approach this practice. We can say this very moment is a Zen Intensive. It is based, it depends, it is supported, by our respons-ability in relationship to our half of the word...

When we talk about the word Zen and the meaning of the word Zen we see more and more Zen as being much more than a practice, and see Zen more as an experience, a living experience, a flowing and unfolding living experience. Seeing it as such, does open really many many gates. And as Dogens says, Zen is the Dharma Gate of ease and joy. And at the same place as an inquiry, an inquiring, deep, formless, daring, fearless inquiring.

Inquiry not being caught up by any fixed form but just inquiring,

Formless deep inquiring into the unknown. As the Unknown herself.

So we can see Zen, as well as Life and relationship, is a practice, and actualization, as well as an inquiry.

The ones who did broke the neo-liberal mirror and war, do also say "Asking questions we walk". **We walk.**

And this walking is contained in a form and community. even if in one moment is is a community of simply an ass and a pillow, a community of two feet and the ground.

The seed is there, and the seed is the tree and the shade. The tree is the rain and the horizon.

So that power, that virtue, that tao, is the Total Availability, total trust, total dedication to the seeds. Yes, in plural, as we are also, plural.

Thus we have this form and this community which is basically the container of that inquiry and play. At that point Zen or Shikantaza or Koan is a living experience renewed moment by moment falling, diving into that **container** of this **form** and the **community** and how it **expresses** outside the limits of the formal place, be it called Zendo or another name in and as our very everyday **life**.

When we say this word "intense" or "intensive" we touch the possible relationship between time and practice and life. And Passion and Love.

Time! such a mystery! As well as practice or life itself. And the question is how do we touch this?

How do we **become** that **intensity**, that **passion** in such a way that that our Attention practice and play, our Zazen and our life is not just hanging in there for the 8 days or 50 or 60 or 80 or 120 years of life?

How do we touch or **how we become, actualize, express that passion,** that intensity without which I don't think we can touch and become intimate with that heart of inquiry and practice.

The notion of continuity blocks that passion to come forth.

In that continuity we lose that passion because we place that ideal time in which realisation or understanding or fulfilment or ease and joy as Dogen defines Zazen will happen, always in the future, always as a projection. Do we by chance do the same with Peace, Justice, Freedom too?

Or maybe we do sit in some kind of formatting or manipulation of the cause, in such a way that we want to produce an effect.

But this I don't think nothing works as well, as bad, we should say, as the illusion of having time, we "think" we have time. Yes tomorrow we continue here?, who knows!!! I don't think so. It may be, it may be not .

And when we fearlessly challenge that security about next moment taken for granted we touch that passion. When we have the illusion of having time, we imagine, we plan, we postpone, that living experience.

So Dogen says Total Complete Dedication, availability to this Tao, this unknown and nameless reality.

So what is practice then? what is play? Is that very Do Toku as Zazen, as Shikantaza, as the "Koan of everyday life", that Koan named as Genjo Koan.

Then those elements, Unconditioned Attention, Full fearless Inquiry, the4 so called Zazen, Shikantaza or the Koan are **expressed as every single step in our life**.

So we have two wings in this practice, there is a lot of emphasis in certain schools about not searching but I think it is also important **not to postpone** that possibility. Not to postpone the horizon, not to postpone the New World, New Heart.

We don't direct ourselves to our aim but also we **don't postpone the potential of this very moment** as the only one for that awakening.

There, with that heart of passion and intensity, that we can call it Zazen or our true nature.

Not to search, not to postpone, becoming one in the simple act of sitting, walking, breathing, living, loving.

In the Taoist tradition the word for Zazen that is used is not the same. The word is used the ideograph that is used is "**Tso Wang**". Tso has the same meaning as Za- sitting. Tso Wang is "sitting in forgetfulness", "sitting in oblivion". Wang is forgetfulness, oblivion, not remembering. So the Taoist tradition which is one of the most important ones in the coming forth of Zen in China. says we sit in forgetfulness, in forgetting us, this act of forgetting everything itself.

Then there is nothing known, thus there is no point of reference.

WE don't know what Zen practice is as we are sitting, we don't know who we are, we don't know what we are and thus as Dogen says the Self is forgotten and all beings from all directions and times come forth and actualise true nature. Actualize the New Heart, New World that is so badly needed on this Blue Planet.

Here then time is our heart and body, space is our heart and body, this brand new living moment is our heart and body. And it is a Common heart and Body, thus, a common walking.

Dogen, in a very interesting essay called Being Time or "the identity of being and time", he says like this: "You may suppose that time is only passing away and not understand that time never arrives. Although understanding itself is time, understanding does not depend on its arrival."

I find this last part quite interesting "understanding does not depend on its own arrival".
We can rest and dance there.

Cheers!!!

"Bowl-Person"

By Augusto Al Q'adi Alcalde

That's the way Rinzai practitioners and warriors did call their ceremonial eating bowl: "Bowl-Person" a strong and inspiring metaphor an engaged for life.

It is beautifully completed by the expression "Oryoki" : 'That which contains what is enough' the way our companions in the Soto tradition do call their bowls.

Bowl Person, That which does contain what is enough...

True Zen practice True Life practice and expression is a full body, is our community in ourselves and with all beings in all time and space.

Many things are happening in the world since last breath.

And I always come to the point in which I remember that the Buddha used to say: only one thing I Convey, how to understand the causes and stop suffering.

Wu Shu, rendered as "Martial Arts" has the implication (in the ideograph "WU") to "stop the sword". the sword that kills, the sword that gives life, says Mu Mon, "No Gate". And when Bodhidharma said "don't know" he was also talking about the sword of Wisdom. Only the "mistery", with "mist". The source of all wonder and creation, says the Old Guy Lao.

That is the vital question. Much more in this moment of the world and humanity and the many beings: to understand the causes of suffering and how to stop it. This by no means I think is an individual task. It is something that we can do, that we can be free completely from suffering if all our fellow beings don't come with us, or we go with them, to that point. Community practice, community body, community understanding.

That, as the Buddha was saying, will be also impermanent, so that this task that should be renewed moment by moment with our whole heart and engaging our whole body, heart and attention as well as our steps. After all, if there are no steps there is no horizon, and if thus, where can the Sun of Limitless Life, Amithaba, rise and shine?.

Lets emphasise in this practice a different kind of practice that has tremendous value. It is a home and everyday based Zen Intensive practice. So our Zen happens at this moment and place and also when we go out of the dojo and go into our everyday life situation. it is thus then pointing and touching the practice of the oneness of our zazen, and our walking kinhin, and our private interviews about practice, and then walking outside and going to our daily work meeting our friends and family members, **as heart-step-practice itself**.

So I see that as the container of practice – that interaction we have with the world at every moment when we are outside this place. So one of the things I would say is please let us pay attention to that ground of practice that would happen in our everyday life and not only when we are sitting on our zafu.

Another element that I think is important for conceiving this is **how, where and when** to draw the line in practice between asceticism and self-indulgence. There is a subtle line there – each one of us knows in his or her heart where the line is. What is for some people asceticism is nothing for others. So please let's draw that line, and let's follow our heart and our body in drawing that line and not our idea or concepts about **how** practice should be. It is a very subtle line. Each one of us knows where is it and it has to be drawn at each moment, each moment, each moment. and we need utter sincerity with ourselves for this.

Secret Practice.

Another element of Zen practice I find fundamental is what I call secret practice. As opposed to what some teachers in our lineage used to say: "stinky Zen". Secret practice, unnoticed practice, a practice that happens in a very subtle way without necessarily shining with fire crackers. Secret practice. So we go outside from here and we do our practice which of course will not be sitting on a zafu with crossed legs, especially if we are interacting with non-Zen people, so to speak. This is secret, but the basic elements of zazen – attention, breathing, posture should be there.

There is one more step about this secret practice that I like to emphasise – that practice that happens and **it even secret to ourselves – we don't notice that practice is happening.**

That is the subtlest way of that secret practice.

And it comes only when that notion of practice as something special, separated from the rest of our ordinary life, dissolves completely. So please, together with the other elements, let us settle in that secret practice in our daily life during the Intensive.

Nothing Special

We said nothing special and I think that is another element of practice. This is just another moment of practice and next breath, next heartbeat we will have just another One Moment Sesshin, forever, beyond time and beyond realization. There is nothing special, here, It is just happening. That quality of "nothing special," just life itself as practice and realisation, is the heart of Zen practice.

I like to quote Dogen when he says in his Shobogenzo: *"to follow the buddha way completely means that you do not have your old views. To hit the mark completely means that you have no new nest in which to settle."* He is pointing to old views and no new nest in which to settle. Sometimes we come to Zen & the Arts with a certain idea about how things should be, how practice should be and what we are supposed to gain from that practice. But Dogen here is saying, you do not have your old views. All those old views, including the one we had a moment ago after our "great realisation and enlightenment experience", should fad away.

We do not have our old views, so that heart and that mind can be renewed moment by moment.

He also says, *"to hit the mark means that you do not have a new nest in which to settle"*. What is he pointing at here? I think he is pointing to a kind of Zen that is the heart path of **inquiring** itself. Not inquiring toward understanding, and not inquiring for some special understanding, but just inquiring as our path, forever, being renewed moment by moment. This is I think what he hints when he says, you do not have your old views anymore.

And he is also pointing to Zen as "walking." We do not have a new nest, we do not practice and then arrive at a safe place and stay there forever. News for you – there is no such a thing. **Zen is walking. Zen is inquiring. Formless walking and inquiring**.

There are certain elements in our practice that do reflect those aspects. We have the breathing, we have the ground of this living moment, and we have the inquiring heart and step. **Breathing** is our companion in whatever approach we choose to come into the world of Zen. Breathing. And breathing implies relationship: we breathe, outside, inside implies that relationship in which the outside and the inside really don't have a sharp line that divide them, so that is an inter-relationship. And that relationship, inter-relationship, happens moment by moment in a flow.

Then we have **this living moment**. We talk about shinkantaza practice as pure attention, pure open attention to this living moment so that actuality will come forth and actualise our heart. This living moment: openness to the unknown, openness to the unexpected, the pregnancy of each moment. Dropping off our old views, we are completely open to that. That comes together with trusting that unknown. Trusting that dark warmth as Lao Tsu points, trusting that pregnancy, that mystery that is our life, moment by moment.

The third element inspires our practice is what we said about **inquiring** itself, as the heart and step of Zen. For that to happen with the "don't know" mind, the mind that is intimate with that mystery, we need to drop certainties; we need to drop attachment to fixed conceptions or ideas about practice. Then what Dogen calls the 10,000 beings as actuality itself advance, confirming the self, actualising the self, making the self, our life, completely actual. Actuality is another key element.

So what can we say about that process, that movement that we call awakening? The Korean teacher Chinul comes to my mind when he says, sudden realisation, gradual personalisation. That is a great phrase and embraces the two aspects of practice. We realise and then we have to **give body** to that realisation, we have to **walk** that realisation. Of course that gradual personalisation happens step by step. But then Dogen has something to say too. He says, **"you may practice Zen forward, but be aware each step is equal in substance"**.

So sudden realisation and gradual personalisation which is that realisation itself taking each one of the steps as an endless, mysterious process. So it is not that we awake through the koan as a means to an end that we call awakening. **It is a matter of embodying the koan**.

Then the koan exists and unfolds in the midst of awakening, **never solved but enriching and inspiring every one of our steps**.

It's a matter of giving body, as in realising the body that is already there, the true body, being one with that body. The body of this very living moment, the body of our nature, the body of our unique life.

We are just as we are, that very heart of practice. Our life as it is, is that very heart.

We are that walking, that inquiring that has the potent capacity of re-creating life at each living moment.

There zazen finds us, embodies us, **as** the mystery as the unknown, as the dharma gate of ease and joy.

Cheers!!!

The Moon

By Augusto Al Q'adi Alcalde

The moon

abiding in the midst

of serene mind;

great waves breaking

into light.

Great waves breaking... just like this moment, this place, realize it or not.
Great waves breaking, our common breath, our common steps, our common horizon.
These are the true qualities of a "serene mind-heart".

"Serene" as great waves breaking into light. Into light-ness.

In moments like this, I feel that there are two attitudes that can come forth in our practice-life.

One of them is to say: "Well, I've been doing it for some time and nothing happened....

What can happen in this single shining moment that we have in front of us? So then we give up, and just use our time to just spend the rest of the day, month, year, life in the best way we can.

The second one is to try to use the "rest" of the time in the best way we can; so, full of anxiety and desperation, we just do our best, or we think we are doing our best.
Then "the rest" becomes "the remains".

But I think the two of them most surely will lead like a heartless arrow to frustration.

The first one, in which we just give up and spend our time taking it easy, doesn't work in the long run. And the other one has tremendous power to accumulate tension, so we begin to be more and tenser as the last bell, the last dawn, the last dusk is approaching us, and also leads to frustration.

So what can we do now?

We can remember Dogen's words and heart about "practising Zen, (full body-mind-heart attention) forward". We should be clear about the living fact, this is to embody-personify that each step, each very step! is equal in substance.

So even though we speak about "joriki", the Vital power and energy, the Ki-Chi of Samadhi, accumulating in a fresh, non cumulative way through days, years, eons of practice-life, and that's true enough, what really awakens the true mind is a vertical movement, timeless, a-temporal and with no space movement, a primal unconditioned movement of full body-heart-mind Attention, moment by moment, whole body and mind, full attention and openness, and please lets be clear about this, with no process.

So lets do not wait for tomorrow.

Complete it right now, moment by moment: finish our breathing, complete our Formless Inquiring with no-cause, that some do call "Koan", just complete our Attention-Heart flashing everywhere.

So that we have nothing ahead, we have nothing below us; just this moment of our common True Nature expressing herself as us freely and unconditionally fresh.

Here we have that poem by Dogen, that says:

> *The moon*
>
> *abiding in the midst*
>
> *of serene mind;*
>
> *great waves breaking*
>
> *into light.*

The moon abiding in the midst of serene mind; great waves breaking into light.

In writing down this poem, Dogen is playing with the meaning of the words and the ideographs.
The ideograph for "moon" here is written slightly differently from the way it is normally done. The ideograph is "tsuki", and in this case, "tsu" means "entire or total, complete, whole" and "ki" means "possibility, capacity, function".

So even though we can still say the poetry is talking about the moon, and it is still written down "moon", it also reads "total possibility", "total capacity", "total function".

Talking about our very lives?
Talking about this moment? Talking about this very heartbeat?

A poem is completed by the one who reads it, so please lets complete it, complete it in such a way that will always be (all-ways) a new step, a new horizon, a new common heart to awake up and embody as a person, "per-sound", does tell me right now this blackbird singing in the dead of night....

That moon, this moon, abiding in the midst of serene mind is the first part of our poem.

I see in this poem a clear affirmation of revolutionary attention, or deep rebel formless inquiring or profound life-practice embodying the Tao of True Nature, call it as you wish.

It's not ever really a method or a certain kind of technology or even approach that we practise; but it is total expression.

So, to quote Suzuki Shunryu, we don't sit or walk or move Zen to "achieve" Buddha nature; we do Zen and thus and then we and I really mean "we" do express fully our Buddha nature.

There is no need for a step-by-step process, even though that walking does happen by itself.

We settle, sink into each step's substance, that equality in substance of each step, of each breath, throughout space of timeless time.

That equality of life-steps that joins our Zen as well as our Life with Shakyamuni's Life & walking and expression and with each one of the ancestors and the many varied teachers of the many Lands who did the creative and revolutionary act of pointing at the moon.

Here our poem shows the dynamic state of "Shikan": from "chih" meaning Samatha or calm openness, meaning "just", and "kuan" coming from vipasyana: attention and inclusiveness.

A very dynamic and creative state, calm moonlight shining, sparkling on ocean waves crashing against rocks and sands as it changes into drops.

Sounds familiar? It is our very life.

This is poetry about the play of sinking into mutual intimate relationship between the light of the moon, the light of total possibility, total capacity, total function, and the dance of all beings, all moments, all situations, all times.

Right there, in our everyday life and practice-expression we find the source of creative engagement in life.

And without that source, without that creative common engagement, there is no life. And that life is not the mere continuation from birth to death, from the beginning to the end, not just that, but as the total experience of birth and death in a single sparkling instant of shedding off body and mind into and as the Unknown.

The visa for entering that pregnant space where we always are, has the "no fear" seal stamped in red ink. Red as blood, as life, as Heart.

Elsewhere, the guy also says: "Birth is just like riding in a boat. You raise the sails and row with the oar

You ride in the boat, and your riding makes the boat what it is.

Birth is just like riding in a boat: you ride the boat, and your riding makes the boat what it is".

No need to say life, our very life and practice, is that boat.

And obviously our riding it makes the boat what it is. Riding in full attention and openness to what the boat is, and how wide and inclusive is, makes our movements right, in the sense of being appropriate to the occasion. Rhythm and the creativity of broken rhythm come forth there as the source of Joy. Like a good dance step for a groovy dance.

How wide is the dancehall?

And the ultimate of that appropriateness is "the 10,000 beings advance and confirm, authenticate, actualize the self".

The so called "self", the boat, the wide and inclusive boat with no rider, the boat made of water, made of waves.

That is true responsibility, that is, the ability to respond. Not the self going forward and naming and handling and manipulating the many beings; but total attention and openness, in such a way that the 10,000 beings, not just one: **all** beings, do advance and confirm, actualize authenticate the "self".

Self as creating, as a common body-heart, as a revolutionary horizon.

The *Genjo-koan* essay, "the formless inquiring into and as ordinary life", has something to say about this water and moon of practice. It says: "Awakening is like the moon reflected on the water. The moon does not get wet, nor is the water broken [shaken]. Although its light is wide and great, the moon is reflected even in a puddle an inch wide. The whole moon and the entire sky are reflected in dewdrops on the grass, or even in one drop of water. Awakening does not divide [shake] you, just as the moon does not break the water. You cannot hinder enlightenment, just as a drop of water does not hinder the moon in the sky. The depth of the drop is the height of the moon. Each reflection, however long or short its duration, manifests the vastness of the dewdrop, and realises the limitlessness of the moonlight in the sky."

The moon reflected in the water: total function, the total function of the body and mind not only shedding themselves off but at the same time coming forth as the brand new fresh shed off body and mind.

Then practice-play as life is complete, in complete engagement with each moment of the heart-mind of the now.
So with the practice of Zen, so with the practice of real Martial Arts, the practice of healing, so with the practice of making a new world and heart, if it has a specific characteristic, it is the practice of total physicality.
Which is to say of Love.

No place for speculation, scheming, manipulation or road map here.

Then there is a certain kind of physicality, of grounding, of concreteness, that is unique. As Love is.

And that quality of practice does come with engagement in "Anicca", which is so-called, one of the three signs of life: "anicca" meaning unconditioned change or transformation; "Anatta" meaning no abiding individual isolated self; and dukkha", translates as something like suffering, but I like more uneasiness".

The spirit and the heart of "not yet"," not yet enough".

Anicca is the fact of life: change and transformation. And our life is engagement with that change.
So we can take a hug from that sign of life, take refuge in the power of this moment, with total heart-mind; take refuge in the power of the freshly new situation coming forth again and again.

No place there for routine or habits or our conditioning mind.

Ready? Lets then invite freedom and Love to dance right now.
"The depth of the drop is the height of the moon".

The depth of the drop is the height of the moon. Really: no depth, no height.

Let us forget the moon, just one drop, coming back home once and again, totally fresh, totally alive, with passion and joy.

Just one drop of total openness, we ourselves are no more there.
Just one drop of full body-heart attention, **that** is the height of the moon.

Moon Earth,
Sun harmonized perfectly
on the bridge
above the vast sea
the mountain echo Path leads me
(says Morihei)

When the Tao, when Love does not fill our whole body and mind, we think it is already sufficient.

When Tao fills our body and mind as them, we understand and feel that something is missing.

Yeah, just like that!!!

When the Tao fills our body and mind, we feel, we understand that something is missing.
But that very thing that is missing is complete in itself.

Let us settle there, let's walk & dance that.

Cheers!!!

"Young Heart, Last kiss"

Notes of a participant in a Zen In Movement retreat led and guided by Augusto Alcalde (Roshi) in the Australian forest.

I want to express here my gratitude and appreciation in full respect to my friend-student-companion of the Way "H. G." for daring to go through the living experience, as well as for sharing her heart.   It is inspiring and encouraging for me, and I deeply hope it will also be likewise for you reading this. Cheers!!!

Augusto Al Q'adi Alcalde

Hello dear zen community. Below are some notes I'd like to share from the summer retreat - its been nice for me to type them up, to remember this not very long ago time as I (try not to) struggle to keep practice alive back home.

With love

H. G.

Sesshin notes

(Sesshin means at the same time "to touch the Mind-Heart, to receive the Mind-Heart, to convey-share-express the Mind Heart")

Coming to the end of the first day and mainly I'm thinking about when I should shower. How stinky am I? Will I do laundry?

And, god I love this hammock. Very profound.

Actually had a nice moment today - before lunch, a shivery awakening feeling and then inspiring thesis thoughts.

Realizing that the Sesshin retreat is an act of love: to myself and to each other. The community supporting, and the ideas justifying this time-space-activity are both acts of love.

Realized this as I wondered: what is the reason for Zen? Why to we/I need Zen? Zen being those things of history, ideas, community.

Feeling the simplicity and love in giving myself time with zazen as activity, released from most demands.

Why does it take zen to allow this experience of just being to reveal itself?

And why does it also take grace - cause a lot of the time you are bored or aching or distracted.

And I feel for the answer in my daily life - back there I haven't been able to sit hardly at all since winter.

Capitalism is a word that comes to mind.

Why Zen? Because capitalism is a force I cannot resist on my own.

Day three and zazen deepens.

Feeling quite natural and close to home.

Yesterday was mainly sleepiness - fell asleep countless times into 30s lucid dreams, heavy heavy eyes. Then evening some feelings: full disappointment at seeing timidity and regrets.

Then full jealousy, envy, fear.

Still trying, practicing the return.

Open available to present moment mind-body-heart.

Thickness and weight in my right chest.

Slept deeply, bright dream images.

This morning - so extremely cold, sat mainly alert.

Image coming of the sky - to be as big and imperturbable as the sky, allowing the massive powers of thunder and lightening to play against your body and to emerge clean, fresh, wide and shiny.

Also helpful yesterday and today: "I don't know."

I don't know if this will be my last heart beat, my last breath.

I don't know because each moment is fresh.

Helpful when I start feeling weighed down by the Sesshin or bored, stiff and sore.

When the lament comes: "how will I get through this?"

I remember that I actually don't know what the next moment of zazen will be like.

"I don't know" keeps the inquiring alive.

Inquiry is like a life line in the everyday world.

Augusto says this inquiry is the heart of Zen.

I feel it is a strong force, a power in its own right, worthy of the forces which seek to master and exploit life.

Went to Dokusan (*private time-space-ground interview and sharing*) in clarity, with just a little bit of fear that evaporated easily.

Shared my experience of a big hard judgment axe cutting through everything.

Augusto said: I hope you have a young heart. A young heart is playful, flexible, creative. It can take risks.

Image came later of the heavy black blade of judgment falling through the open expanse of blue sky - just falling, no harm done, nothing in its way.

Today, day four, grumpy day.

Last night a massive rush of panic and anxiety about my dog.

Worry close to childhood abandonment fear deep in the pit of my belly, close to the spine.

A terror: how can I leave this place, this Sesshin? How can I go back to my life?? Day five.

After lunch, sitting in my most divine hammock (thank you friend who packed it in my things). Much easier today morning.
Took some great advice from Dokusan last night about cycles and rhythms, trust in impermanence etc.

Good to voice my frustration and see it for what it was.
Today practiced with that and avoided trying to hold on to good sensations, caught myself trying to push for a particular state.

Aaaah practice is so much easier than effort!
And affirming context and perspective: so, right now I am stuck and can't feel any wonder or movement.

Don't resist it.
Have noticed sleepiness functioning as a backlash after an intense bit, suspect that heavy stuckness might be this also.

To remember is also protection.
And from Dokusan, most helpful idea: **sudden realization, gradual personalization. Insight experience leaves, but leaves a trace and then you have the work (or joy) of fitting it into daily life, looking at all its facets, ramifications etc - like a jewel says Augusto, that's the interesting part.**

Lovely lovely little moment today as I suddenly realized the wonder of breathing. Breathing.

The whole world of living creatures taking air into their cells, air which is energy coming in and flowing out.
I heard a bird sing and I could feel her breathing.

I saw the oceans breathing, the whole planet pulsating on the infinite textures of its breath.
Awesome. Wonder.

And I looked right up then (as I wrote this) to see an eagle circling.
Awesome. Wonder.

I know that I've never felt that before, never truly asked the question: what is breathing? Awesome.
Wonder.
But now, of course, and directly after, the feeling has gone.

Good thing was I remembered to let it go and as it passed I felt joy and lightness.
Still I'd like to bring it back, there is that desire in this recording here.
But instead can I explore what "gradual personalization" might mean?

To turn it over and around and let light reflect on its many facets, without suffocating or exploiting it, without trying to squeeze the juice out of it.
This must be something different.

From the Teisho (Talk on the Heart of Zen): **"let treasure be treasure and it becomes giving."**

Day six. Back to the slog.

Lots and lots of distraction today, thought trains running express.
Lots of making plans for my new flat, but just about anything would do.

Bit of shame, fear envy stuff on kinhin (walking meditation) but mainly just busy, busy, busy thoughts. Caught myself this morning and focused some strong dedication. Resorted to naming thoughts: "future pleasure" etc.
Thus especially now as the world pressure gets close that I want to practice with commitment. it is hard though.
Last sit was especially tough, knees aching and irritation from the flies and just blasted distraction and waiting for the bell.

Tried to be with all that.
Have been noticing something about layers and distance.

About not going forth but just being here, in place. Get tempted to say waiting. Not waiting but practicing not interfering, nothing extra.

Got some little glimpses on this - feels powerful but hard to grasp. Of course grasping is exactly not the point.
Augusto said about treasuring those blessed moments, he imagined it like the last kiss he would give his lover if he were dying - very soft, gentle.
Resonates with my image of the little bird's fluttering chest.

Anyway, last full day. It has been overall really gentle, well paced, well supported.
Feel very happy...

NIGHT BROTHER's Zen (Ch'an) Way

Augusto Al Q'adi Alcalde (Roshi):

Nyo'ei Gen'un Ken

Augusto Alcalde is an Argentinean Zen teacher with the Chin Lien Chia (of **Chan-chnese Zen**) and one of the first Dharma Successors of the late **Robert Gyo'un Aitken Roshi**. He also was fully authorized as a Zen teacher by his first teacher the Monk Yuan Chueh in the year 1974.

An social change activist for much of his life till the present time, Alcalde-Roshi grew up in the small jungle town of San Pedro de Colaláo. He was a militant member of the anarchist-libertarian scene from 1965 to 1976, a form of political activism which eventually put his life in jeopardy because of the military dictatorship ruling the country then.

During this time, from 1967 to 1978, he was a student of the late Shih Fu Yuan Chueh, of the Po Yuan Temple, an exiled Chinese monk who was living in Brazil, from whom he learned Traditional Chinese Medicine, the Chinese Internal Arts of Movement and Martial Arts, and Ch'an (Zen) practice, according to the Chin Lien (Golden Lotus) School of Chinese Buddha and the Tao ways, in the Huang Pei family tradition.

Authorized to teach by Shih Fu Yuan Chueh, Alcalde founded a Zendo and taught at the Chinese Yoga and Martial Arts school in 1974.

In 1978 he began studying with Robert Aitken-Roshi of Diamond Sangha and he moved to Hawaii to study more intensively. He was made an apprentice teacher in 1984 by

Aitken-Roshi and became his attendant when traveling to other areas of the USA and other foreign countries.

In 1986 he returned to Argentina and founded the Shobo An Zendo in Cordoba hills, as a continuation of the old Vimalakirti Sangha, then fully affiliated with the Hawaii Diamond Sangha.

In 1989 Aitken-Roshi traveled to the Zendo and led a training period and Sesshin, giving Dharma Transmission to Augusto Alcalde in conclusion.

He lives at the Autumn Bridge Dojo, and directs the "Cultural Corner Inn", a house for Zen practice, rest and health and a center of Traditional Chinese Therapies. This place is open for residence around the year, and instruction is available in both English and Spanish, and visitors are very much welcome.

He teaches Learning the Tao with the Body ("Shingaku Do"-Dogen Zenji) which is the practice of the Chinese Internal Arts of Movement of the Nei Ch'ia Chuan Shu, in the context and ground of traditional Zen and the Tao practice.

It is an expression of the teachings of the late Shifu Yuan Chueh of Po Yun Temple, Canton, and the Chin Lien Chia, the "Golden Lotus" Ch'an (Zen) school (of the Complete Realization Lineage) and the Shifu Augusto Al Q'adi Alcalde (Roshi) who is fully authorized as a guide and successor in the lineage by Yuan Chueh in 1974.

Augusto, responding to the suggestions of his teacher, Robert Aitken Roshi in the Oahu Island of the Hawaii Nation, reintegrated the Internal Arts of Movement to his own teachings into the Soto-Rinzai Zen lineage, in which he is a Dharma successor himself. He taught and guided retreats, intensives, meetings and practices in the Zendos and Dojos of the Hawaii Nation over the years. He teaches in Argentina, Chile, Mexico, Hawaii and Australia as well as in other places on this wounded Mother Earth, also through what he calls his Cyber-Dojo and Matrix Sangha.

In 2000 Alcalde resigned from Diamond Sangha Buddhist Society and continues his work inside the Harada-Yasutani Lineage and the Chin Lien Chia bloodline of Chinese Ch'an.

Contact and info:

Saludrebelde@yahoo.com.ar

http://autumnbridgedojo.blogspot.com.ar/2011_02_01_archive.html

https://www.facebook.com/augustoalcaldezenenmovimiento?ref=hl

https://www.youtube.com/user/ZenenMovimiento

20974608R00071

Printed in Great Britain
by Amazon